# JOI BANGLA!
## The Children of Bangladesh

Jason Lauré
with Ettagale Lauré

# JOI BANGLA!
## The Children
## of Bangladesh

Photographs by Jason Lauré
Farrar, Straus and Giroux | New York

To Asia Jasmine and the children of Bangladesh,
who made this book possible and necessary

Library of Congress catalog card number 74-14394
ISBN 0-374.3.3780.2
Second printing, 1975
Printed in the United States of America
Published simultaneously in Canada by
McGraw-Hill Ryerson Ltd.. Toronto
Designed by Cynthia Basil

Photographs on pages 15, 16, 17, 18-19, and 21 by Jason Lauré | UNICEF

# Contents

# JOI BANGLA!
## The Children of Bangladesh

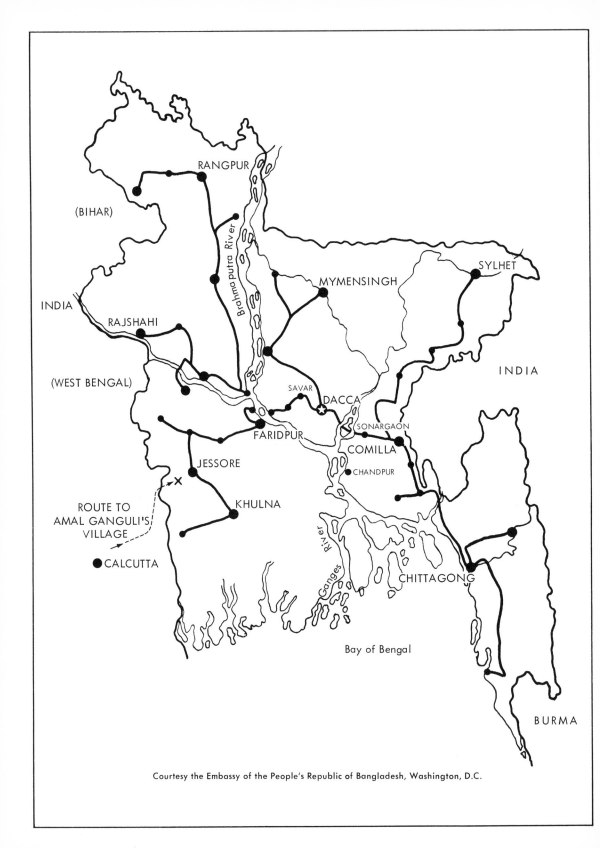

RANGPUR

(BIHAR)

Brahmaputra River

INDIA

RAJSHAHI

(WEST BENGAL)

MYMENSINGH

SYLHET

INDIA

SAVAR

DACCA

SONARGAON

FARIDPUR

COMILLA

JESSORE

CHANDPUR

X

ROUTE TO
AMAL GANGULI'S
VILLAGE

KHULNA

CALCUTTA

Ganges River

CHITTAGONG

Bay of Bengal

BURMA

Courtesy the Embassy of the People's Republic of Bangladesh, Washington, D.C.

# Foreword

The history of modern Bangladesh begins in 1947, when the British empire of India achieved independence.. Because of religious strife, the land was partitioned into two countries, India and Pakistan, Hindu and Moslem respectively. But Pakistan was a geographical impossibility—a nation created by committee. Its two sections, East and West Pakistan, were separated by nearly a thousand miles of Indian territory, united only by their Moslem religion.

The physically imposing West Pakistanis speak Urdu, are light-skinned, and are closely aligned to the peoples of the arid lands of the Middle East. The more delicately built, dark-skinned Bengalis speak Bengali and have much in common with the inhabitants of the humid countries of Southeast Asia.

Although East Pakistan contained a larger share of the population, the central government was located in West Pakistan. All decisions made by the government favored West Pakistan at the expense of East Pakistan, which contributed 55 to 70 percent of Pakistan's foreign-exchange earnings, largely based on the jute crop, while receiving only a small allocation of government monies in return.

West Pakistanis totally dominated the government and held virtually all key posts in the military, the civil service, banking, and business as well. Insistence on use of the official language, Urdu, effectively kept Bengalis from assimilating into high positions. In 1952 the frustration of the Bengalis erupted in language riots. Supporters of the teaching of Bengali were arrested and imprisoned for intellectual crimes. One of the most vocal Bengali supporters, a law student at Dacca University, would later become the embattled leader of Bangladesh, Sheik Mujibur Rahman.

East and West Pakistan coexisted uneasily for more than twenty years. In 1969, when General Yahya Khan became president, he promised free elections and a return to civilian rule, and in December 1970 Pakistan's first national general elections were held. The results dealt a crushing blow to West Pakistan's dominant position.

The Awami League, a political party that appealed to the uneducated peasants, won 167 of East Pakistan's 169 seats in the Constituent Assembly. The Awami League's charismatic leader, Sheik Mujibur Rahman, known widely as

Mujib, now began negotiations with Yahya Khan and ex-Foreign Minister Zulfikar Ali Bhutto, head of the Pakistan People's Party. The three met frequently in Dacca, capital of East Pakistan, from the time of the elections through nearly all of March, ostensibly to form a new government. But the negotiations were simply a stall to keep Mujib from exercising his power. Yahya Khan did not have enough West Pakistani seats to remain in power. The outcome would be a Bengali prime minister in the person of Sheik Mujib.

Unwilling to allow this, General Khan reverted to his military training. On the night of March 25, 1971, he let loose a massacre of the people of Dacca. With no warning, and no opportunity to defend themselves, Bengalis were shot on sight by the Pakistani soldiers, wherever they were found. Students in their beds, merchants in the markets behind their stalls, people on the street—all were shot. The bazaars and shopping areas were set afire. Those who were trapped inside died in the flames; those who managed to escape were shot by the soldiers.

This action, called the "crackdown," was a massacre of defenseless people. The students were the first target of the troops and tanks that invaded the city, for they were the traditional source of political agitation in East Pakistan.

The killing went on all night. In the middle of the night, Sheik Mujib was arrested and taken to prison in West Pakistan. He remained there, a symbol of Bangladesh's struggle for independence, for nine months.

On the second day of the crackdown, the soldiers moved into several areas of Dacca, including the old section, where most of the Hindu population lived. For hours they worked to destroy as much of the "old town" as they could, burning homes and shooting anyone who tried to escape. That night, troops roamed the streets with local Bengali collaborators who pointed out the houses of Awami League workers. These houses were then destroyed.

On March 27, the curfew that had been placed on Dacca was lifted. Almost immediately, people began leaving the city. Within the next forty-eight hours, thousands fled. All told, an estimated nearly ten million people left their homes in East Pakistan, seeking sanctuary in neighboring India. This endless stream of refugees, most of them Hindu, put an intolerable strain on the economy of India, which faces a constant struggle to feed its own people. This strain would later prove to be a key element in India's decision to step into the conflict.

Soon after the crackdown, the people of East Pakistan, although leaderless with Mujib imprisoned, declared themselves to be the independent state of Bangladesh, a name that means "Bengal nation."

For the next few months the West Pakistani soldiers continued their massacre of the Bengalis. The crack forces of the central government, numbering 80,000, who were stationed in East Pakistan quickly seized control of all key points in Bangladesh. During this period, the only serious opposition

the West Pakistani troops faced was from the East Bengal regiment in Chittagong, the second-largest city in Bangladesh. These trained soldiers later formed the nucleus of the Bengali Mukti Bahini, the liberation army.

The East Bengal regiment escaped from East Pakistan into the hills of India for training. By midsummer they were organized, and they returned to begin a counterattack on the West Pakistanis. They blew up Pakistani ammunition supplies and conducted raids.

Once the Pakistani soldiers began to move into the countryside, they resorted to guerrilla warfare. Atrocities were committed by both sides, and the war dragged on through most of 1971. Additional troops continued to arrive from West Pakistan throughout the war.

Although West Pakistan's hold over East Pakistan was shaky, President Yahya Khan and his advisers believed the rebellion would fade out eventually and there would be a return to prewar conditions. At this time, they held control of the urban centers at gunpoint, but 90 percent of the population is rural.

By the end of November, the refugee situation in India had become desperate. With its own population of 560 million, India could not afford the burden placed on it by nearly ten million refugees. In the state of West Bengal, situated next to Bangladesh, conditions were intolerable. Seven million of the refugees had crowded into camps there, vying for jobs in Calcutta with West Bengal's own impoverished millions.

India had another reason to enter the war on the side of the struggling Bengalis. Twice in the years since partition in 1947 it had gone to war with Pakistan. If it could win freedom for the Bengalis, India would be assured a friendly neighbor on its eastern flank. The 1,300-mile border between India and East Pakistan would no longer need protection. Pakistan would be reduced to its western wing, losing an estimated 60 percent of its population and 55 to 70 percent of its foreign exchange. The weakening of this country would leave India the dominant state on the Asian subcontinent.

Border skirmishes between Indian and West Pakistani troops in Bangladesh had occurred during the fall of 1971; on December 3, 1971, India moved openly against the West Pakistanis. Bringing in heavy air support, it staged a major battle against the vastly outnumbered West Pakistanis. During the first week, India bombed Dacca airport, putting an end to West Pakistani reinforcements and supplies.

Although the Mukti Bahini had gained strength during the late summer of 1971 and continued to fight through the fall, it was India's troop strength and aerial attacks that changed the war from a guerrilla action to a decisive military victory. On December 16, 1971, the West Pakistani Army surrendered to India and the civil war was over. Bangladesh proclaimed itself the world's newest, and eighth most populous, nation.

---

*Bhabishat Bahini, the children's squad of the Mukti Bahini*

On December 14, when it was clear that defeat was at hand, the al-Bahadur, a group of Bengali Moslems with fanatical religious ideas, launched a senseless massacre. Seeing the two wings of Moslem Pakistan about to be separated irrevocably, they rounded up three hundred of the budding nation's intellectuals, torturing and killing most of them.

On December 16, 1971, newspaper headlines proclaimed:

"DACCA FALLS." It was at the historic moment of the West Pakistani surrender that I arrived in Calcutta. As a journalist, I was eager to witness and cover the emergence of Bangladesh.

Calcutta, a teeming city of seven million, in the province of West Bengal, had provided temporary refuge for millions

of Bengalis during the war. These victims of the fighting lived in subhuman conditions in the refugee camps. As soon as the war ended, they began to head back to Bangladesh, the homeland they had dreamed of, to begin a new life. I intended to enter the new nation of Bangladesh with some of the first returning refugees.

At the camp I met Amal Ganguli, one of the refugees. Like many educated Bengalis, he speaks enough English for us to hold a conversation. He came from Bhandubila, a quiet little village about thirty miles from the Indian border. Amal, a Hindu, is a member of a religious minority in his country. The West Pakistani soldiers showed no mercy to the Bengalis, though most were their fellow Moslems, but they meted out the worst treatment to the Hindus, a traditionally despised religious group. Life in Bhandubila became too dangerous for Amal, a widower, and his three children. They made the perilous trip to India and for seven months occupied a tiny tent in a Calcutta refugee camp. They endured the heavy rains of the monsoon season, which turned the entire camp into a filthy, disease-ridden hell. Sharing their misery were hordes of people of all ages with nothing to do but wait for the next food handout.

I had gone to that part of the world to record in photographs and words the birth of a new nation. What better way to do it than actually to walk back with the people themselves? It is a rare privilege to be an eyewitness to history in the making.

14

Amal's family and I shared the road back with thousands upon thousands of returning refugees. Like Amal, they had been living for long, desperate months in the filthy, wretched camps, thrust together into inhumanly small living areas. Amal considered himself fortunate, though, for his children were with him. Many other families were separated forever during the rush to get out of East Pakistan.

The returning refugees were jubilant. All along the way they sang and shouted the joyous cry, *"Joi Bangla!"*—"Long live Bangladesh!" Everyone was smiling and excited, though they had no idea what awaited them. But they looked forward to a brand-new life. We walked along a beautiful, tree-lined road that made the people feel like a triumphant, conquering army instead of the ragged, hungry band they actually were.

16

On my walk back to Bangladesh with Amal, we enjoyed warm, dry weather. At night we slept along the side of the road, under the stars. Though Amal spoke very good English, his children spoke only Bengali. I taught them a few words of English and they taught me some Bengali. They would always laugh when I first pronounced a Bengali word. Then they would say it correctly again and I would repeat it. The walk back took four days, and all the way Amal and I talked.

Our most serious concern was what Amal would find when he looked for his house. What he found proved to be far worse than either of us could have imagined. All of Amal's hopes were crushed when he looked at the wreckage of what

had once been his home. The roof was gone and the interior completely gutted. Vipers and cobras had built nests in his living room. His farm animals had been slaughtered and his coconut trees destroyed.

When we crossed over from India, Amal had decided to
bypass the clearance house at the Bangladesh border where
officials were distributing clothing, blankets, a small amount
of cash, and a two weeks' supply of food. Amal felt that the
two-day wait to get the allotment might prove to be un-
necessary if he found his house in good shape. But now we
had to go back for the vital provisions. Having returned to
Bhandubila with Amal, I spent a few more days with his
family and then went on to Dacca, the capital of Bangladesh.
That was the last I saw of Amal. By now he should have
received the farming tools and medical supplies promised
by the government to help him build a new life.

As soon as I arrived in Dacca, I found a room in a pension,
a private home with rooms to let, where some relief workers
were also staying. Since the pension was in a residential
section of the city, I arranged for my mail and messages to
come to the Intercontinental Hotel, a gathering place for
journalists from all over the world.

Whenever I went to the hotel to pick up my mail, I
noticed a girl selling flowers just inside the parking-lot gate.
She seemed to be there all the time, always with a big smile
on her face. I often bought flowers from her, exchanging a
few words of English or Bengali. It was surprising to see such
a young girl out on the street, especially at night, and I often
wondered about her safety and what the future held for her.

Early in January, Bangladesh's legendary hero and only
true leader, Mujib, was released from jail by Pakistan's new

president, Ali Bhutto. During Mujib's nine-month imprison-
ment, he had had no news of the war and of his people. He
was allowed neither newspapers nor a radio. On January 10,
1972, he returned to Dacca and rode through the streets from
the airport in a flower-bedecked truck. A half million of his
countrymen filled every inch of space to cheer Bangabandhu—
"Friend of Bangladesh." It was a hero's return for the man
who had inspired the Bengalis.

After about four months of work in Bangladesh, I began
to feel the need to return home to America. The new nation
continued to struggle for survival, but my work seemed to be

21

at an end. But the children of Bangladesh haunted me. How many were there like the flower girl? I wondered. I saw young boys peddling bicycle rickshaws through Dacca's dangerously crowded streets. Wherever I went, I saw children working. They were the future of Bangladesh, but what did the future hold?

I longed to tell the world about these children and their lives. A nation reveals itself through the uniqueness of the individual, the drama of a single life. Wars do not happen to a nation; it is individuals who are devastated by disaster. It was my dream someday to do a book about these young people of Bangladesh.

Back in New York, my work kept the images of Bangladesh and its people constantly before me. As another year passed, I began to plan a major trip around the world, the core of which would be a return to Bangladesh. Many questions haunted me as I made plans. Would I see any of the people who had been such an important part of my life there? What had happened to the flower girl? What was life like for the children?

When I arrived back in Dacca, I headed straight for the Intercontinental Hotel. As soon as I had checked in, I contacted a friend who works with one of the local relief agencies. Through him I met a twenty-two-year-old college student, June Alam, who was to act as my interpreter. He quickly earned both my admiration and my friendship as we traveled around Dacca and its environs, talking to the children who appear in this book. Fluent in Bengali, Urdu, and English, June proved to be an invaluable partner as I fulfilled my dream of the previous year. Together we found children who represented the many strands of Bengali life. And, incredibly, we found the flower girl who had charmed me so the year before. Her life had grown more difficult in that year, but her smile never vanished. Her story is the first chapter of this book.

*Joi Bangla!* Long live Bangladesh!

*Jason Lauré*
*New York City*
*March 1974*

# 1

## ASIA JASMINE
### eleven
### Flower girl

Asia (pronounced *Ah-zee-uh*) is her real name, Jasmine her nickname. She represents the strength, the hope, and the history of Bangladesh. At the age of eleven, Asia functions as the sole support of a family of nine. With a quick, clever mind, a brave spirit, and an instinct for survival, Asia sells flowers on the streets of Dacca. The money she earns, perhaps two hundred *taka* a month (about twenty-seven dollars), buys some food and pays the rent for her entire family—three sisters, three brothers, her parents, and herself.

Asia began her career shortly after the Pakistani Army cracked down on the Bengalis, on March 25, 1971, the so-called night of the generals. With Bengalis being shot on sight, Asia's father was afraid to go to his job. The family's income stopped—but their need for food and shelter did not.

With incredible courage and imagination, Asia began her dangerous work as a flower girl. "In order to go downtown to sell my flowers, I had to get past the Pakistani soldiers, so I would pose as a Bihari girl." The West Pakistanis were sympathetic to the Biharis, with whom they have many common bonds, including the Urdu language. Asia spoke their language well enough to answer their questions and satisfy them with her answers. "The soldiers often asked me where the Mukti Bahini [Bengali freedom fighters] were. Of course, I always denied knowing anything about them."

It was a great risk for her to go out at all, and especially to talk to the soldiers. She was risking her life, but to Asia the path was clear. The family had no other source of income. Her youth benefited her, because the soldiers were not so hard on a child as on adults.

"The soldiers themselves would buy flowers from me," explained Asia, "for 10 or 15 *taka* [$1.50 to $2.00] a bunch. In this way I began to earn a bit of money to bring back to my family. Without it, we might have gone hungry for days. I used to take my flowers to a shop that sold shish kebab, near the army camp at the airport. Soldiers would gather at the food shop to have a bite. This was an excellent place for me to do some business. I earned between 200 and 250 *taka* a month."

After independence, with the Pakistani Army no longer in Bangladesh, Asia shifted her flower-selling operation. "One day I found myself near the Intercontinental Hotel. The foreigners—especially the journalists—bought many flowers from me and gave me a lot of money for them. I saw that I could earn far more selling a small bouquet to an American or a European than to a fellow Bengali. I'd stand just inside the grounds, near the parking lot. I could count on earning an average of 15 *taka* a day, enough to support my whole family."

But sometime after she found this prime location, the security guard from the hotel began to harass Asia. Impressed with his own uniform and position, he tried to extract bribes from her to let her stay on the premises. "He told me I would have to pay him 7 or 8 *taka* a day, half my earnings, if I wanted to continue to sell my flowers there. Of course, I couldn't afford this—I would have no profits left at all—so I

retreated to a position on the main street, just opposite the Intercontinental. But the opportunities here are not nearly so good and my income is only about half what it was before." This has put a severe strain on Asia's family, for she estimates that they need 350 *taka* a month to live decently. Still, the 200 *taka* that she makes is all they have, so even this reduced amount is welcome.

Asia goes to school each day and does chores at home before beginning her flower selling. "The flowers I sell are bouquets and garlands that I buy ready-made at the flower market. There is a variation in price, but they usually cost me between 5 and 7 *taka* each. I ask for about 10 to 15 *taka* for a bouquet—that is the price I can get from a foreigner." She cannot sell to the Bengalis because they could not afford this

price. "I go to work about five or six o'clock in the late afternoon, first going to the market to buy my flowers for the day. Some days I buy about 15 to 20 *taka* worth of flowers." This part of her work is a gamble, because she doesn't know if she will be able to sell all that she buys. "On some days the customers do not come and I cannot sell all the flowers I have bought. On such a day I may finally give them away. Ordinarily I stay out until seven or eight o'clock in the evening, but I may be out as late as midnight, if I am having a slow night."

Although she is afraid to be out that late, Asia feels there is no choice. If she doesn't earn money, there is nothing to eat. Always waiting for her at home are her hungry family, hoping she will come back with money for food.

Asia's father accompanies her every night when she goes to buy her flowers. While she is selling them, he is always standing nearby, keeping a protective eye on her. Unable to get a job himself, he is very ashamed that he cannot provide for his family—and he is especially humiliated to send his young daughter out on the street to earn money for the family. But all he can do is watch over her from a discreet distance.

Asia experienced the thrill of her life when Sheik Mujibur Rahman, prime minister of Bangladesh, came back to Dacca from prison on January 10, 1972. He returned to a hero's welcome. "I remember that day perfectly. There was a great parade and I stationed myself among the crowd. My flowers sold like hot cakes because all the people were in a very excited, holiday spirit. Just at that time Mujib came by, and I presented a big bouquet to him. He offered me money, which I did not want to take, but he insisted."

Asia is beginning to be challenged by some boys who are selling flowers too. Since she is still the only girl, foreigners seem to prefer to buy flowers from her—but the days of her monopoly are over.

Asia is a Moslem, and in the religion of Islam, flowers are held to be one of the few things the Prophet loved. To Asia they are a sacred gift of heaven, and selling them is a sacred occupation.

"Sometimes I get frightened," says Asia. "One night a man, who was probably drunk, snatched the flowers from my hand. I resisted him and tore a chain from around his neck. Another man stepped in to help me and said, 'Why are you taking the flowers from this poor girl? You have no right.' There were other witnesses, too. Then I gave him back the chain and he left."

Asia is deeply concerned about her oldest sister, Mauvia. The night of the crackdown, when the Pakistani soldiers were at their strongest, Mauvia was kidnapped and taken away by them. Many girls were taken by soldiers to be raped and kept in the army camps. The family does not know if Mauvia is dead or alive. They got two letters from her, from Karachi, Pakistan, after independence. She wrote that she was all right and would return to Bangladesh when she is permitted to, but it is unlikely that the family will ever see her again. She may have been forced to write the letters. Girls like Mauvia, who is said to be very beautiful, never return to their families. Even if there is an eventual repatriation of prisoners, these girls are considered to be dishonored. Those not killed by the soldiers disappear, many of them into slums where they become prostitutes or beggars. No Bengali man would want to marry such a girl.

Although the Pakistani soldiers are Moslems like Asia, she thinks of them as infidels because they came to suppress the Bengali Moslems. Her home was in the midst of the fighting and shelling. "We lived very close to the cantonment, near the airport. I was very frightened by all the shelling, and I would take my flowers and find shelter inside an empty water tank. But I went out to try to sell flowers whenever I could."

This was the time when Asia was posing as a Bihari girl and speaking Urdu to the soldiers. "One day the soldiers brought me to my father to question him. He began to speak Urdu, which he speaks very well, and so we were able to keep up the pretense that we were Biharis." Asia managed to pick up more Urdu by hearing the Pakistani soldiers talking among themselves. In the same way, listening to foreigners in Dacca, she has picked up some English. She manages to teach herself what she needs to know.

Asia had good reason to be frightened of the soldiers. "One day I saw Pakistani soldiers passing by in a truck. They stopped two young Bengali students, brother and sister, and caught them by the hair. The soldiers began to beat the students with their rifle butts until they fell on the ground, bleeding from several wounds. Then the boy was shot by the soldiers. The girl was taken away in the truck." Probably she was raped, becoming one of the Biranganas, the "affected women" or "heroines," as they are called. Asia feared that the same thing would happen to her, but she was saved by posing as a Bihari and because she was too young to be of interest to the soldiers.

"I also saw the dogfights between the Indian and Pakistani aircraft, and I was very afraid of that, and of all the shelling. My whole family would get together and pray for our salvation."

When the bombing intensified in December 1971, near the end of the war of liberation, Asia's family went back to Faridpur, their native village. This is the area that Sheik Mujib comes from. "Because we had no money for transportation, we walked all the way back to Faridpur. The journey took us three days. In order to get food for the trip, we had to sell everything we owned." They came back to Dacca in January, just before Sheik Mujib returned.

Since liberation and the release of Sheik Mujib, Asia has had great hopes for her future and the future of the new country. And the routing out of the Pakistani Army has meant that they can live in safety. But her happiness always remains marred by the thought of her sister still being held in Karachi.

34

Asia has only two sets of clothes, both of which were given to her by foreigners who saw how much she needed them. She cannot afford to buy any clothes, which are now three and four times more expensive than before independence.

Asia's home, rented for twenty *taka* a month (three dollars), is a miserable hut, a kutcha house—that is, much worse than second-class. "My whole family—mother and father, brothers and sisters—all sleep on one bed and a *tatami* [straw] mat, spread on the dirt floor. When it rains, the water comes in, turning the floor into a muddy mess. This tiny, miserable house is not a suitable place for the family, and we want very much to move out. We would like to move to a better house in Dacca, but it is impossible, since rents are so high." With her reduced income, they cannot think of moving at this time.

"We get our drinking water from an outside tap used by many people. We must also go there to bathe and wash our clothes. Though there is water just in back of the house, a sort of lake, it is not good water and cannot be used. For lighting in the house, we have a kerosene lantern."

Asia's daily diet and that of her family is very simple and typical for Bengalis. "In the morning we have *chapatis* [a kind of griddlecake made of unleavened wheat flour]. We may have tea with it, if we can afford it that day. If not, we just eat it dry. This would be eaten early in the morning, about seven o'clock. In the afternoon we have rice. At night, it is *chapatis* again, since rice is very expensive. Wheat is cheaper than rice and so we have it twice a day. Occasionally, when I can afford it, I buy some fish or meat at the market, but this is rare. When I was still working inside the grounds of the Intercon [the popular name of the hotel] and my monthly income was higher, we had much more money to spend on food. Then we ate more meat and fish."

Though Asia is a very intelligent girl, she is only in the third grade. In better circumstances, she would be in grade six, but she must pay for her own education and so has had to delay her schooling. "Each month I must pay fifteen *taka* to attend my school. Although there is a free school, I don't think it is worth going to. The students are not very attentive and the teachers do not teach properly. There is a lot of noise, and not really very much education." So she pays to go to a school that offers a real chance at education. Asia is in school

four hours a day, from nine in the morning until one. Although she studies English in school, she has learned most of the English that she speaks from talking to foreigners.

Asia does not have all the books she needs because she cannot afford to buy them. Sometimes she borrows books from her classmates. In spite of all these handicaps, she likes to study and knows that if she had been able to start school earlier, she would be in a much higher grade. If she could earn more money, she would spend some of it on a house tutor, someone who could guide her and speed up her learning. This would cost perhaps twenty to thirty *taka* a month. Asia still hopes to finish her basic schooling and go on to college. And her ambition is to be a journalist.

"Journalism holds a great fascination for me," she says. This is very easy to understand, since she was in an ideal position to observe the comings and goings of journalists during the war of liberation and in the months following. Though Asia cannot afford to buy a newspaper to read, she understands what a journalist does. "If I become a journalist, I'll be able to move around a lot and go to foreign countries. There I can cover the news and do fact-finding." Perhaps because she has seen so many newspapermen, she has a strong desire to travel. She would like to go to those countries which are, for her, dreamlands. "I think I would unravel many secrets there and find out things for myself." Unlike most of the young people interviewed, Asia does not want to stay in Bangladesh. If she finds a country she likes, she says, she would settle down there, for she feels that she cannot move around freely in her society without being criticized. In Western societies, she feels, there is much greater freedom— and being a reporter will help her to fight for others' freedom. Her view of America is of a land of happiness, where there is no sorrow and no pain, a dreamland where everyone is happy and enjoying life. Her judgment is based on the behavior of the Americans as compared with that of the Russians. "The Russians rarely buy my flowers. The Americans often do, and they give me much more money for them." The Americans have "too much money," she notes. Her insights are astonishing for an eleven-year-old.

"One day while I was still selling flowers at the Intercon, a popular Bengali movie star, Olivia, stopped to talk to me. She asked me why I was selling flowers and I told her about my family. Then she offered me a film-acting career." Asia's parents were totally opposed to this, however. In Bangladesh, being part of the film world is considered to be less than honorable. Though she could have made a great deal of money, her reputation would be forever tarnished. Surprisingly, Asia was not at all disappointed when her parents would not give their permission; she has the same outlook as her parents. She believes that their decision is the right one for her; her reputation is more important than the money she could have made. This attitude is firmly engrained in the people, and though Asia is quite a liberated young lady, clearly there are limits to her thinking.

Though she bears her burden with an ever-present smile, Asia is conscious of the gap between herself and her classmates. Most of them have many of the material things she would like to have, as well as the opportunity for schooling. They have the books she needs for her studies. And she is embarrassed because she must sell flowers, a loss of social status.

As a result, and because she is older than her classmates, Asia has few friends among them. And because she is so worldly, it is natural that she would have friends much older than herself. Indeed, her best friend, a sixteen-year-old girl, has just married and now leads a different kind of life. So Asia is very much on her own.

What little time she has for recreation she spends with her brothers and sisters. She says she can hardly imagine enjoying herself, having fun and vacations like other children. And she is always worrying about her kidnapped sister.

If Asia is ever to escape her burden and have more time to spend in school, her family must find other income. One way would be for her father to run a small shop, selling rice and other basic foodstuffs. A grocery shop like this would cost about fifteen hundred to two thousand *taka* to open. It would bring in an average of twenty *taka* a day, or enough to support the family comfortably.

Whether or not the shop becomes a reality, soon Asia must stop selling flowers. "I know that when I have grown up a bit more, and am beginning to fill out and look more like a woman, it would be improper for me to be on the street selling flowers." She would be in danger of being molested and would certainly earn a bad reputation. Every day brings Asia closer to the end of her career as a flower girl and brings her family closer to losing its only means of support. No one knows what will become of them once Asia Jasmine becomes a woman.

# 2
## MOMIN ULLAH
### sixteen
### Rickshaw wallah

The promise of the city shines bright for a boy from the country, a boy who has become a financial burden on his father. And so, at the age of fourteen, Momin Ullah set off on a difficult and dangerous journey to Dacca, that glittering beacon of hope.

He left his village of Delaiy in the district of Noakhali with five *taka* (less than one dollar), money that he had earned selling coconuts and betel nuts. From Delaiy, about seventy-five miles southeast of Dacca, Momin Ullah walked three miles to the station and took the train to Chandpur. From there he went by steamer (launch) up the Meghna River. He continued his journey for a while on land, by bus. Then he boarded a steamer again, arriving at the ferry ghat (landing) in Dacca. Although the shortest way from Noakhali to

Dacca is only about seventy-five miles, he was obliged to take this circuitous route because of the disruptions that had occurred in Bangladesh during the war of liberation.

In the low-lying, flat Bangladesh countryside, rivers form a network of travel routes. Many of the bridges spanning these rivers were destroyed during the war, forcing travelers like Momin to break their river travel and go part of the way on land.

Momin showed great courage and ambition in making this trip alone, just a few months after the war, but it could scarcely have prepared him for his desperate struggle in the ruthless environment of Dacca, a city that already held too many people competing for too few jobs. Because his journey had consumed his savings, Momin spent his first day in Dacca without food. Imagine arriving in a large, crowded city, a city where you know no one and have no prospects for a job and no money. Then imagine that you have no skills and very little education. What terrors must have crowded his mind as Momin spent those first twenty-four hours hungry and alone in the city he hoped would be his salvation.

"My first impression of Dacca," he says, "was of a very fascinating place, but after a couple of days I found out that it is only for rich people; for poor people who don't have any money or any job, it is certain death and starvation and miseries."

After that first terrifying day, Momin had a stroke of good fortune. He met a kind man from his own district who gave him some money and food and found him a job in a teashop, serving tea and cakes.

For two months, this slight fourteen-year-old boy toiled for sixteen hours a day—from six o'clock in the morning until two o'clock in the afternoon, then from four o'clock until midnight—earning about twenty *taka* a month (just under three dollars) and untold abuse from the habitués of the tea-shop. After working this wearying schedule, he had no bed to look forward to. Instead, he considered himself fortunate to be allowed to sleep on the table of the teashop after it closed for the day. Finally, when he could no longer tolerate the terrible hours, poor pay, and mental and physical abuse, his benefactor again stepped in and taught Momin how to drive a bicycle rickshaw, or pedicab. He found the boy a job as a rickshaw wallah, pedaling through Dacca's teeming streets. With so many men competing for a few positions, Momin was lucky to have someone get any sort of job for him.

In developing countries, only bureaucrats and the wealthy have cars. Travel by bicycle rickshaw is common. Indeed, in Vietnam the Ho Chi Minh trail was kept open by the trans-portation of matériel by bicycle. People in Bangladesh travel long distances by rickshaw. Actually, little alternative exists. During the war of liberation, many of the buses were de-stroyed, and the few that are left are very crowded.

Since he was fourteen, Momin has followed his trade as a rickshaw wallah, earning about twenty to twenty-five *taka* a day. Out of this he pays ten *taka* a day to rent the rickshaw.

Momin is quite young for the exhausting job of a rickshaw wallah and must compete with men both older and sturdier than he is. These tough rickshaw wallahs try to prevent him from taking foreigners on board; foreigners are usually charged twice what a Bengali can pay. But Momin has become self-supporting and actually manages to save some money—fifteen to twenty *taka* per month, which he sends to his parents, two brothers, and two sisters in his native village.

What did Momin expect when he arrived in Dacca? Hope loomed large in his mind when he left home. The promise of the new nation of Bangladesh was great. The beloved leader, Sheik Mujib, had given the people great inspiration.

Momin says, "I expected to work in some government officer's house, for someone who was a financially secure person. I thought I could work as a servant for some time, and then perhaps persuade this officer to find me employment somewhere. I hoped in that way to earn some money to send home to my brothers and sisters for their education, and to improve the financial situation of my family."

This dream quickly vanished. Reality in Momin's life begins each morning around three when he gets up after the call for prayers and walks a quarter mile to the place where the rickshaws are kept. By four o'clock he is making his way around the city, looking for passengers. Within four hours he has earned some money, and stops to buy his breakfast, *chapati* and perhaps a meat curry. After this meal he continues to work until two in the afternoon. When his ten-hour

shift is over, he returns the rickshaw to the owner, who rents it out for a second shift to another driver. One part of his life has not improved since he worked in the teashop: he is still sleeping on a table, this time in another shop. He has no pillow, nothing to soften the hard surface of the table.

Although Momin appears to be wearing a *lungi*, a typical all-purpose garment, in fact he has taken another garment, a *chaddar*, and just wrapped it around himself so that it looks like a *lungi*. It is tied in a special knot in front. In the knot he ingeniously keeps his money, for he has no pockets, nowhere else to put it. He is barefoot. He has no other possessions except one shirt and one old pair of trousers.

In these circumstances, health conditions are brutal; predictably, Momin was stricken with a severe form of dysentery. For nearly three weeks he suffered a high fever and dysentery. He was unable to go to a hospital, and his savings were completely wiped out by the cost of the medicine he needed—forty *taka*. He had to borrow eighteen *taka* to make up this sum. After his recovery he started back to work, burdened with debt.

Once back on his feet, Momin continued to ply the streets of Dacca, looking for passengers. On Sundays he tries to earn extra money by cruising around the movie houses which have morning shows. Here he can earn as much as twenty to twenty-five *taka*. Sometimes he'll station himself in Motijheel, the busy commercial area of Dacca, when the office workers go home. Or he'll pick a spot where there are few choices of transportation, like the narrow, congested alleys of the city where neither auto rickshaws nor cars go. (Also called the "baby taxi," the auto rickshaw is a motor scooter with a bench added on in back for the passenger.) His instinct for finding fares is very good by now.

Momin is obviously an intelligent boy—one can see it in his eyes. His answers during a five-hour interview were very direct and he did not hesitate once in answering a question.

48

This is the tragedy, for, with education, he could give much to his country. His education stopped after the fifth grade and he cannot think of going to school any more, although he realizes that with a better education he could get a better, less strenuous job.

Because there are no meters or set rates for rickshaws, Momin must calculate the cost of each trip as it occurs. He gets some of his information from the older drivers, and by now has a good idea of the fares to most of the usual places. But when he takes a passenger to a place where he has never been, he leaves the fare up to the honesty of the passenger. In effect he is saying, "You travel this route every day, you know it better than I do." This works out well, for Momin says that people are generally fair to him. Some are very sympathetic and will pay more than he asks because he is so young.

Compounding Momin's financial worries is the danger of an accident. There is no insurance to cover personal injuries or damage to the rickshaw if a wallah has an accident involving a car. He can try to beg something from the driver or passengers in the car to pay for damages, but often, because owning a car represents a higher station in life, the driver disclaims responsibility and flees from the site of the accident. So the rickshaw wallah has to bear an additional burden that he can ill afford. If he has a flat tire, he must pay for the repair himself and of course loses valuable work time while the repair is being made.

Every day Momin Ullah's main concern is just staying alive. What he earns in a day determines what he eats. For lunch he might have rice with a curry, either vegetable, beef, or mutton. (Since Momin is a Moslem, he would not have pork.) But if he can't afford that, then he will have *chapati*, which is much cheaper than rice, and with it some *dal* to flavor it. For supper it will be *chapati* and curry again. He spends an average of four *taka* a day for food.

Momin's one day off, Saturday, is a day for renewing himself. "I try to get much sleep then and to eat well. And in the evening I go to Dacca Stadium to see a football [soccer] match. Every Thursday night I go to High Court to listen to the Bauls of Bengal singing."

The Bauls of Bengal are the underground folk heroes of the nation. Closest in spirit to gypsies, they wander the country, carrying with them the songs of the people. In the festive atmosphere of the gathering at High Court, Momin enjoys a respite from his week of toil. "High Court" is the general name for a park that contains a legal court, as well as a large open area where many groups appear, to entertain. Occasional cigarettes or *bidis*—cheap cigarettes made from coarse tobacco—provide another small pleasure for him.

Before he left his home for the uncertainties of Dacca, Momin experienced the horrors of a war fought on his land, in his own village. He saw his house destroyed by the enraged Pakistani Army. Most of the other houses in his village were burned down by the army, which suspected that there were many freedom fighters there. Because the villagers did not respond to the soldiers' questioning, the houses were burned. Momin knows that one of his uncles was a freedom fighter, but fortunately no one in his family was killed, although a few people from his village were.

But, as was typical in this war, many of the beautiful young girls of the village were kidnapped, taken to cantonments, and raped by the soldiers. These girls have disappeared from the village, probably never to return. Some were killed in the camps, some committed suicide, some were taken to West Pakistan, where they were kept in captivity. For some of these women, a solution was ultimately found in government abortion clinics, established precisely to handle the situation of the "affected women," the Biranganas.

For Momin Ullah the success of the Mukti Bahini in liberating the country was a surprise. He thought, and quite rightly, that the Pakistani Army was much stronger, that there was no chance of winning. This feeling was intensified when a local representative of the Pakistani Army was put in charge of the so-called peace committee. This representative, or commissioner, was a local Bengali who was expected to collaborate with the Pakistani Army, letting loose a reign of terror in the village.

But in Momin's village the commissioner was shot dead by the freedom fighters. Other collaborators, seeing their own future, changed their identities and joined with the

Mukti Bahini. Because the Indian Army did not come to his village, Momin did not realize at that time the large role it played in the success of the war of liberation.

By the end of the war, though, he knew of the fighting between the Pakistani and Indian armies and was sure that the Indian Army's strength had enabled his country to achieve independence.

What of the glorious promise that brought Momin Ullah to Dacca? "I thought that if the country was liberated and if everything came into our hands, then there would be fantastic progress and prosperity and the country would flourish. Everyone would smile happily. I thought things might be much better in Dacca than in my village, and that I could have a better life there."

But to his utter dismay, the situation is just the reverse. Prices—even of essential commodities—are three times higher than they were during the Pakistani rule. Momin's situation is miserable. Austerity is the rule he lives by, the only reality he knows. The promises have not been kept.

In the first two years of his life as a rickshaw wallah, Momin was able to see his family only twice. His isolation is especially heartbreaking in a land where family ties are so important. But the trip is both long and expensive and the time spent at home is money lost. So he looks forward eagerly to the one or two letters he receives from home each month. Infrequent mail service intensifies his separation from his family.

Religion, which plays such a large part in the life of the Bengalis, carries with it its own responsibilities, and even these cannot be met by Momin Ullah. "I am religious," he says, "but I can't pray regularly the way I did in the village. According to the basic rules of prayer, one has to be very clean, to dress properly, to cover the body properly. I don't have nice clothes, clean clothes, so I pray in my mind. In an unconventional way, I am communicating with Allah."

Far off in the future, so far that he cannot yet really envision it, Momin Ullah expects to marry a girl selected for him by his parents. He is very firm in his conviction that she should be a girl from his own village: "A girl from Dacca wouldn't be obedient; she wouldn't be loyal or sincere to me. I could not be peaceful in my mind. But if I marry a girl my parents choose from my own village, then I would have nothing to worry about. She would always stay indoors and wouldn't communicate with other people."

Marriage, though, is not even a remote possibility for him. Only when his brothers and sisters are well established financially would he consider marriage. As the oldest of five children, Momin may in this way be avoiding the reality of his bleak future, for he cannot truly expect to be able to provide for his entire family.

But even a boy like Momin Ullah dares to dream. He dreams of owning his own rickshaw and renting it out to other drivers. From the profits, he could buy a second rickshaw, and so on. But this dream has little substance, since a new rickshaw costs about two thousand *taka*. Added to that are the costs for registration and the many expenses that seem

to mushroom in bureaucracies. The total would be perhaps twenty-five hundred *taka*. He would have to save this money before he could buy the first rickshaw. Yet, as he pedals through the streets of Dacca for another long and exhausting day, he holds the dream in his mind.

# 3

## SHAHIDA BEGUM
### eleven
### Beggar girl

"Rich man, poor man, beggar man, thief . . ." What child doesn't know that old rhyme? But who knows a beggar girl, a real girl? What of Shahida Begum, an eleven-year-old Bengali girl who roams the streets of Dacca, begging to earn 2 or 2½ *taka* a day?

No one seems to know just how Shahida began to beg. No one asked her to beg, however, and though her closest friend is also a beggar, it's unclear whether her friend influenced her. Shahida says that it all happened out of simple necessity. One day there was no food at all, she had no proper clothes, and so in desperation she just set out to beg in her rags.

Many sad and diverse elements combined to create Shahida's extreme situation. Her natural father, whom she loved very much and who returned her affection, died of cancer when Shahida was a small girl. Her stepfather, a kind of vagabond, stays at home for a month, then goes away for a month or two, and then repeats the pattern. When he is away, no money comes in at all. But even when he lives at home, he spends most of the earnings from his job as a rickshaw wallah smoking and drinking intoxicating country liquors. Shahida's mother is unable to go out of the house because she has no decent clothes. And her brother, who is learning to be an automobile mechanic and thus represents a ray of hope for the family, at the moment brings in no earnings.

In addition, the family occupies a wretched but expensive house. More realistically called a hut, it is constructed of straw and bamboo canes, with a roof of straw. Yet for this inferior house, the rent is ninety-five *taka* a month (thirteen dollars). And should the family fall one month behind in rent, as often happens because of their shaky financial situation, they are threatened with eviction. There is no lease involved in these houses—they are rented on a monthly basis.

And so, at ten years of age, Shahida became desperate to help her family and herself and set out to beg. This was a very difficult task, for she is an extraordinarily shy child. She feels terribly humiliated because she has been forced into this position. Her embarrassment about the begging is painfully evident. Still, she goes out almost every day to try to get some money from the people on the streets.

Shahida's closest friend is Shalima, who lives next door. They are such good friends that Shahida uses the word *shakhi* in referring to her, rather than *bandhu*. *Bandhu* is the word for "friend," but *shakhi* denotes a very special, close relationship. In the morning the two girls go begging in their own neighborhood, Ajimpur, although each tries her luck on a different street. Shahida's workday begins at nine o'clock. "I stay out on the street all morning, until about one or two in the afternoon. Then I go home for something to eat. At five in the afternoon I go out again and head for the New Market [an important shopping district]. At New Market there is a big crowd of shoppers, rich Bengali people and foreigners." Shahida has learned that the foreigners are more generous in their handouts. "In addition to money," she says, "sometimes I get some old clothes or a bit of rice or some other food. There is a tremendous rush of people here, and many cars. This is the best place to beg." Shahida stays no later than eight o'clock in the evening, because she is so young and should not be out too late by herself. She goes to the New Market every day except Friday, which is a holiday.

The first time Shahida set out to beg, she felt very pessimistic. "I thought that people wouldn't give me any money, but all the time I was thinking of Allah, and relying on Him. I know that whatever Allah does is the best for us. I leave everything to His mercy."

When she is begging, Shahida invokes the name of Allah,

saying, "Sahib, I am a poor girl, I have no food and no clothes. So please give me some money, in the name of Allah. Allah will be kind to you." This appeal helps Shahida to attract attention. When people do give, the amount is perhaps five or ten *paisa* (one or two cents). In her simple view, Shahida sees those who give her alms as being kind and good, while those who do not are rude and not good people.

After begging for a few months, Shahida's pessimism faded and she became much more optimistic about her chances. "Now I know I can expect to get more money than when I first began to beg. And I also get more gifts of food and goods." Shahida hopes that her family's financial condition will improve, especially when her brother gets a job as a mechanic. At that time she expects to stop begging. She thinks he will earn enough money to look after her so that she can go back to school.

Presently, Shahida's only schooling consists of an hour's religious instruction in the morning. "Every day I go to a Moslem mosque. There I learn to read, write, and speak Arabic, and especially to read the Koran, the holy book of the Moslems. Also I am taught how to say my prayers properly, five times a day." Shahida's family all honor Mohammed, the great Prophet of Islam.

Because the family had to move from the area where her school was located, Shahida's schooling ended. (She can read

---

*Shahida, with Shalima and Shahida's blind uncle*

only the Bengali alphabet and can scarcely write at all.) At that time she was only six years old and no special facilities existed for destitute and orphan children. These programs have since been instituted, but Shahida doesn't have decent clothes to wear in order to attend school. Nor can she afford to buy the books she would need—books are not furnished free, although, under the new regime, there is free schooling up to the sixth grade. The tiny amount of money she earns by begging must go to buy things more essential than books, such as a little rice. Shahida remains optimistic about returning to school. In the meantime, she attends the Moslem school each morning before she sets out to beg.

Shahida traces both her unhappy situation and her family's hard times to the time her father died. "I still cry when I remember his affection and all the love he showed me. Now I feel very lonely most of the time." Her stepfather does not treat her badly—he doesn't beat her—but he is very inattentive. Shahida greatly needs attention, warmth, and affection. Although her mother does love her, she too is unable now to show her affection for her. Shahida's uncle arranged the marriage between her mother and her stepfather, thinking it would improve the family's situation. It proved to be anything but beneficial to them, and her mother is now helpless to improve her miserable life.

Shahida's afternoons are the most pleasant part of her day. "When I return home after trying to earn some money, I help my mother prepare lunch. Sometimes I have been given

some rice or vegetables by a kind person and we eat that."
They might have a vegetable curry, but not one with meat.
They cannot afford meat. "After lunch I like to go out to play
with my friends. Usually we skip rope. Later, when I go back
to my house, we have our evening meal, which is just *chapati*
and *dal*. Sometimes there is no *dal*, so we just eat dry *chapati*
and drink water with it. I must go to bed very early because
I have to get up at five o'clock in the morning, when it is still
dark." Then she begins another day of religious instruction
and begging on the streets.

Shahida, like most of the young people in Bangladesh,
expects to marry when she is in her middle teens. And, true
to her upbringing, she expects the marriage to be arranged.
The idea of a love marriage is never considered. Romantic
matches are alien to the life and thinking of the people.

The total deprivation of the family can be seen in the torn
old dress Shahida wears. It was given her by her landlord.
Now the back is virtually gone from the dress. The bangle
bracelets she wears, called *churi*, were a gift from her brother.
Her earrings and her copper necklace were given to her by
her mother, who received them from Shahida's father.

During the nine-month period of the war of liberation,
Shahida lived in a slum area. She remembers some of the
terror of the time. "There was not much fighting in our area,
but one day I saw a boy being caught and blindfolded by
the soldiers. Then I saw him shot twice in the back. I was
very frightened."

This was a very difficult time for the family. Shahida was afraid to go out. The family faced extreme financial hardship, with almost no food from time to time. Somehow, they just barely managed to stay alive. Though only eight years old at the time, Shahida knew that her life was in danger. She prayed to Allah for the safety of the Bengali people and the freedom that they hoped for.

Though she was too young to comprehend what the new nation of Bangladesh meant in patriotic terms, Shahida understood that in such a new nation the people could ex-

pect more food, more clothes, more money. There would be growth and prosperity.

But her high expectations for a bright future withered away. Now she must face her tragic situation: almost no food, no clothes, and no money. And instead of a loving father to comfort her, she must suffer a stepfather who, at best, shows only indifference toward her.

For Shahida, the foreseeable future rests in the hands of her brother. When he becomes an auto mechanic, he stands a good chance of getting a job, for technically trained people are in very short supply in Bangladesh. Though much of the country lives in poverty, there is a layer of bureaucracy complete with imported, chauffeur-driven vehicles. Mechanics are needed, and the salary Shahida's brother will earn should enable him to help his little sister. Then, perhaps, she can end her time of begging and return to school and a more normal life.

# 4

## SARWAR ALI
### fifteen
### Bihari boy

In the days before the war of liberation, life was pleasant for Sarwar Ali. His father, a manager in an important steamship company, provided a comfortable life for his large family. Sarwar, his two brothers, and his five sisters enjoyed their life in Mohammedpur, then a very pleasant section of Dacca.

Suddenly, civil war erupted in Pakistan and Sarwar found himself "the enemy." Sarwar's people, the Biharis, came from the state of Bihar, in northeastern India. A Moslem minority living in a land of Hindus, the Biharis chose to emigrate to East Pakistan when the Indian subcontinent was partitioned just after World War II. (Most of the Indian Moslems were located in the areas that became East and West Pakistan.)

So Sarwar's family came to the city of Dacca more than

twenty-five years ago to enjoy life among their fellow Moslems. Many Biharis were granted concessions by the Pakistan government when they arrived in the late 1940's because they brought with them needed skills. The Biharis, unlike their new countrymen, the Bengalis, spoke Urdu, a separate language. In physical appearance there was also a difference between the Biharis and the Bengalis. The Biharis maintained these differences, marrying within their ethnic group, and never integrated with the Bengalis. Their allegiance was with the West Pakistanis, who also spoke Urdu. When the war of liberation broke out, many Biharis collaborated with the West Pakistanis, earning the enmity of the Bengalis.

The night of March 25, 1971—the night of the crackdown—Sarwar and his family left home and stayed away until after about a week's fighting, the Pakistani Army had secured the area and it was safe to return. Like all the Biharis, Sarwar's family was well treated by the Pakistani Army and was supplied with rations and all they needed. This assistance was to cost the Biharis dearly. When the liberation became reality, the Bengalis took revenge on the Bihari people, some of whom had betrayed them. Hundreds of Biharis were slaughtered; some of the Bihari girls were taken away and raped. Sarwar's brother was arrested and jailed, but was later released. Today Sarwar and his family live as strangers in their adopted land.

Thousands of Biharis, dwelling in various parts of Dacca, headed instinctively for Mohammedpur, to be with their

kinsmen. As the war progressed, they poured into Mohammedpur, turning this once-lovely section into a ghetto. The
population grew tenfold. Suddenly squatters were putting up
tents or simply living in the streets. Where there had been
homes, there were now encampments, as this enormous increase in population overwhelmed the area. Streets became
open sewers. Heavy rains flooded the area, covering everything with mud and silt. From this time, Sarwar has lived as
a member of a threatened minority.

In addition to the excellent job Sarwar's father held, the
family's income derived from three grocery shops they owned.
These were taken over by Bengalis, as were most of the
houses in the area. Although Sarwar's father complained to
the Bangladesh officials, their sympathies were with their
fellow Bengalis and they refused to correct the situation.
Sarwar and his family managed to keep their house. It's the
only thing they have. Now they are surrounded by Bengalis
who came to the area immediately after independence, taking
advantage of the confused situation to move into the former
homes of Biharis.

Perhaps the worst effect this disruption has had on Sarwar's
life is the change in his schooling. He had attended a pukka
school, one that offered a full matriculation. Had he continued there, he would have earned his first qualification,
considered the first milestone in an academic career. But
Sarwar is too frightened to go to that school any more.

"I am very much afraid that I would be beaten up if I

tried to continue to attend my old school, which is located outside Mohammedpur. Now my education is continuing at an Urdu school." The teachers at this school are non-Bengali, like Sarwar. But this school, which stops at the junior-high level, is a makeshift affair, not up to the academic standards of the other. This is Sarwar's last year there; he is completing the highest grade his school offers. It doesn't even have a proper building, but occupies part of a mosque, so classes have to be suspended during prayer services. But for Sarwar there is no choice, for there is no high school in Mohammedpur and he dares not go outside the area alone. The best he can hope for is to be tutored at home by his brother-in-law, who lives with the family, and by his father.

Sarwar's life centers around his school days. "I begin school at nine o'clock in the morning and attend for three hours." Many activities in Bangladesh begin early and end early in order to avoid the devastating heat of midafternoon. "I study Bengali, English, Urdu, and mathematics." The emphasis on languages, three subjects out of four, points up the dilemma of his life. Although Sarwar speaks Urdu at home, he must speak Bengali when he is outside Mohammedpur. This is not only to make himself understood but to avoid trouble, for Biharis are not welcome in the Bengali community.

"When my classes are over for the day, I go home to do my homework. I usually meet my friends in the afternoon to play football and just pass the time in gossip, idle talk." Sarwar has very little to occupy his time. He would prefer to

74

play hockey but does not have the money for a ball and stick. In the evening he may study, then have his meal, and go to sleep about nine o'clock. Sarwar still counts some Bengalis among his friends, although inevitably they have drawn apart. His former school friends no longer come to his area to visit.

The effect of the war on Biharis like Sarwar is a total disruption of the life they once knew. From comfortable, middle-class life they have fallen into absolute poverty. All their possessions were taken by the Bengalis. "I was in the house when people came with guns and threatened to shoot me. At gunpoint they took everything. We had nothing to say—we had no weapons. They said, 'You have helped the

Pakistani Army, you have given it assistance, and now we are going to take care of you. We're going to finish you off.' "
This looting took place in broad daylight.

The shirt Sarwar wears was given to him by one of his friends. The looters left him without a shirt to wear. This shirt and his trousers are the only clothes he has. He doesn't even have a pair of sandals or shoes. Though no one in his family was beaten or tortured physically, the Bengali robbers left them with barely the clothes on their backs. Sometimes his sisters and brothers cannot go out for lack of clothes. Outside of a few schoolbooks, Sarwar has no possessions at all.

Having lost the excellent job he held before the war of liberation, Sarwar's father attempts to keep his family together with his earnings from a part-time job on a ferryboat. However, his salary of two hundred *taka* a month cannot be stretched to meet the most basic needs of eleven people. So they take loans to buy food and hope for relief food. Although the family is supposed to receive weekly rations, sometimes they come two or three weeks late.

The rations that finally arrive consist of *atta*, a kind of wheat in the form of flour or meal. Unlike the Bengalis, Biharis are not rice-eaters. Wheat forms the basis of their diet. From the wheat they make *chapatis*. For most meals, this is the only food the family have. They eat the dry *chapatis* three times a day. When they can afford tea, they moisten the *chapati* with it. When they can manage it, they have some vegetable curry.

"Sometimes, when my father gets his salary, we have a beef or mutton curry. It's a very big occasion to have a meal like that now. Mostly, we are just managing to live."

Should Sarwar's father lose his job, the family would be forced onto the streets as beggars, because they have no one to help them. They might be able to sell their house for five thousand *taka*. The house has two rooms, with inside plumbing. If that were gone, they would truly have nothing.

Once outside the encampment of Mohammedpur, Sarwar poses as a Bengali to assure his own safety. Although he used to go out alone, now he won't risk it and goes only with his parents, perhaps once or twice a month. He speaks as little as possible outside so that he will not reveal that he is a Bihari. When he does speak, it is in a very low tone for fear that his accent will betray him. Whenever Sarwar goes to downtown Dacca, he is nervous and insecure.

Sarwar is most comfortable speaking Urdu. When interviewed, he spoke Urdu with the interpreter, an educated Bengali who is fluent in both Urdu and Bengali, as well as in English.

The situation for the Biharis changed somewhat for the better during the first year after liberation, giving them a slightly greater feeling of security. But Sarwar does not expect Biharis and Bengalis to coexist comfortably in the future. "I could never think of settling down in Bangladesh. I would always feel insecure here and wouldn't think of getting married and having children."

The majority of the Bihari community—those who lost their businesses, their prosperity—would like to leave the country. For them, the dream is to go to Pakistan, a country more sympathetic to their religion, their language, their total life-style.

But repatriating to Pakistan would cost more money than a family like Sarwar's can hope to save. And even if they were able somehow to get the money to travel, they would still be blocked by the Bengali Bangladesh government, which does not issue passports to non-Bengalis. It is an irony that the Biharis are not wanted in their adopted country, yet are not allowed to leave for the one place that is sympathetic to them. (It is doubtful, however, if the Pakistani economy could support an endless influx of Bihari refugees.)

The Biharis have been denied passports for political reasons. It is thought that they will be kept in Bangladesh as long as there are Bengali prisoners of war in Pakistan. The Bengalis are not finished with the punishment of the Biharis who collaborated with the Pakistani Army. Sarwar, though only a boy, has been caught in the middle. He, like most of his community, is a victim of the war.

Some Biharis do get out. Shortly before the interview with Sarwar took place, his uncle started the long, risky journey to Pakistan. Corruption is not unknown in Bangladesh, and for those who have money, a passport can sometimes be arranged. However, getting out of Bangladesh is not the end of the journey. Sarwar believes his uncle has managed to get as far as Nepal, where, for the moment, he is stranded. He must then find his way into Pakistan, hundreds of miles away. Whatever the dangers of the trip, it is still considered a better risk than staying in Bangladesh.

Some of Sarwar's Bihari friends embarked on this perilous journey, escaping from Bangladesh and reaching Nepal. Others have completed their journey and are now living in Pakistan. Sarwar receives letters from time to time, telling of their new life there. His dream is to follow those friends. He doesn't know how he would manage it—he doesn't know exactly how they went—but he wants so much to go. Sarwar is both dismayed and comforted by the fact that these boys were even younger than he—some only thirteen years old.

If he should ever get to Pakistan, Sarwar hopes to live with his uncle. He thinks he would have no problem continuing his education and would have a chance of an academic career. Such a hope is out of the question in Bangladesh.

But, unlike his friends, Sarwar wants to go to Pakistan with his entire family. Though he has no hope of a job, he dreams of earning enough money to finance not only his trip but that of his family: mother, father, brothers, sisters, and brother-in-law. He wouldn't go alone, he says, even if he earned the money for his own trip. Perhaps it is no more unrealistic to dream of taking all eleven people than of escaping by himself.

# 5

## PRATHIVA RANI ROY
### twelve
### Hindu girl

Hindu in a Moslem land—that's the story of Prathiva Rani Roy. In 1947 Pakistan was created to contain the Moslem people who were unwelcome in India, a land of Hindus. But the lines drawn to partition Pakistan and India overlooked pockets of Hindus. Thus Prathiva's family, like many other Hindus, has lived as an uneasy minority for years.

During the war of liberation, Prathiva and her family (her mother and her two younger sisters) fled their home, hiding from the Pakistani Army. They were fortunate enough to be hidden by friendly Moslem families who lived in their village of Sonargaon. Most Hindus left Bangladesh entirely during the civil war, escaping to India. But Prathiva and her family had nobody to guide them from Sonargaon to the Indian border, which is a great distance away, nor did they have the money to travel. Their only recourse was to keep moving about from place to place, taking shelter with Moslem friends. They stayed in remote places to escape the Pakistani Army. For the nine months of the war, from March to December 1971, they were continually on the run.

Their situation was complicated by the presence of the *razakars*, the "storm troopers" of the Pakistani Army. These were local Bengalis, and in some areas Biharis, who collaborated with the Pakistani Army, working as informers in exchange for money, food, and clothes. One of their tasks was to ferret out the Hindus who were hiding. If the Pakistani soldiers suspected that they were members of the Mukti Bahini, they were killed. Some Hindus in Sonargaon were killed by the soliders, and some of the women were raped. But Prathiva, her mother, and her two sisters were able to elude the Pakistanis and came to no harm during the war.

The Pakistanis singled out the Hindus because they were thought responsible for the mutiny of Bengal from West Pakistan. The soldiers believed that the Hindus had a secret contract with the Indian government. Although the Hindus certainly did not have such a contract, India's sympathy toward them was inspired by the desire to have a friendly neighbor to the East, rather than a hostile nation. When it became clear that the Bengali people needed outside help to win their fight for freedom, India stepped in, and within two weeks brought the war to a successful conclusion for the Bengalis.

For Prathiva, the war came as close as her house. "While we were hiding from the Pakistanis, the soldiers sometimes came to the house where we were staying. Then I would pose as a Moslem girl." Although there is no difference in appearance between the two religious groups, and no discernible difference in dress, their names are quite different. "When I was asked my name by a Pakistani soldier, I would say that it was Rahima Khatoon. This is a typical Moslem name that I chose for myself." No one taught Prathiva to say this. It was just a natural expression of her intelligence and instinct for survival.

The soldiers could have pressed the point by asking her to eat meat, for Hindus of her caste eat no red meat at all. "If I had been threatened by the soldiers or if they doubted that I was really a Moslem, then I would have been compelled to eat meat. For me, this was absolutely a matter of life and death."

For Hindu men, the question of religious affiliation can easily be proven. Moslem men are circumcised, while Hindu men are not. But for married women, the only outward sign is the red paint used along the part in the hair, called the *sindur*. This, of course, would be left off in times of war when identifying oneself as a Hindu could mean death.

"We were helped to keep up this pose by the people who hid us. Whenever possible, they would vouch for us as Moslems. They would say that my mother and sisters and I were part of their family."

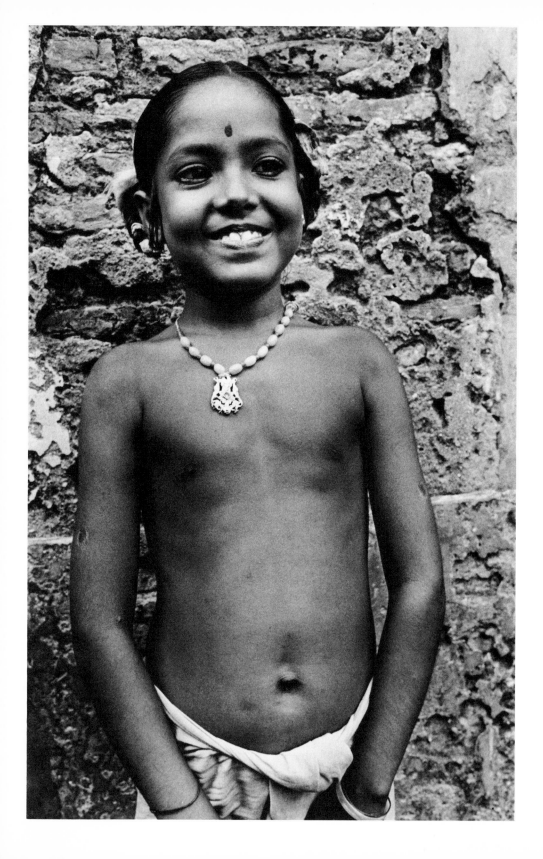

During December 1971, at the very end of the war, when India stepped in, the road leading to Sonargaon was mined by the Mukti Bahini. "All of us were instructed by loudspeaker not to go near the street; live mines had been placed there and we might be killed if we crossed this road." When a convoy of Pakistani Army trucks passed over the road, many of them blew up. "I heard the sound of the tremendous explosion when the convoy went over the mines." Immediately afterward, the Pakistani Army sent in reinforcements to take revenge on the people of the area. Several people in the village were killed during this time, but the freedom fighters staged a very strong counter-action. Many of the Pakistani soldiers were killed, and the rest retreated. For Sonargaon, and shortly for all of Bengal, that was the end of the war.

When the Hindus escaped to India during the war, they abandoned their houses. The people left behind moved into them. Although just empty shells, they provided shelter for those who had no homes at all, or who lived in even poorer huts. It is in such a house that Prathiva and many members of her family live. Although it is quite roomy, there are few amenities. To get drinking water, for instance, they have to go to a well 250 yards away.

Prathiva's father, who had been a factory mechanic and craftsman, died of cancer when she was eight. Now the family's only income is from the eight bighas of land they

_Farida, one of Prathiva's neighborhood friends_

own. They allow other people to till this land and grow rice and vegetables on it. When the crops are harvested, Prathiva's family receives half the crop. They keep some of this harvest for their own use and sell the rest in the marketplace. This brings them a small income.

There is a marked difference in the way the family lives now. Before Prathiva's father died, they had better food, better clothes. Prathiva had money to spend on amusements. Now she has only the dress she is wearing, no other clothes. Some of the things the family did have were sold to buy food and other necessities. So they live from day to day, on their earnings from the crops.

This land has been in Prathiva's family for a long time. "I'm not sure how many generations of our family have lived in Sonargaon. It has been very long, though. My grandfather and his ancestors all lived in this same place, which is the ancient capital of Bengal. I think perhaps my grandfather once worked in the court of the sultan, many years back."

There are few Hindus living in this village now, so most of Prathiva's friends are Moslems. She says there is no strain in her relationship with these children. In her school, nearly all the young people are Moslems—there are only twenty-three Hindu children. Prathiva and one boy are the only Hindus in her grade.

Prathiva has a few schoolbooks that were given to her by the Bangladesh government. She also has some books for which she had to pay one or two *taka*, out of her own pocket.

"I expect to be able to complete my schooling up to the tenth grade and matriculate. I would like very much to go on to college [comparable to the last two years of an American high school], and then to the university, but I am afraid there is little chance this will happen. There is no one who could finance my education." Although at the time of the interview, a plan was being considered to provide free education through the tenth grade, as yet Prathiva can count on free schooling only through the first five grades. From grade six until matriculation at grade ten, she must pay seven *taka* and thirty-five *paisa* (one dollar) tuition each month. And although there is scarcely enough money to feed the family now, Prathiva says that her mother's friends will see that her basic education is properly completed. This system of matriculation at grade ten was established by the British during their rule over India and it remains in effect today. If the government's plan for free education through grade ten becomes a reality, Prathiva's two younger sisters, aged ten and four, will benefit.

For now, Prathiva spends six days in school, including Saturday. "I study five subjects: English, Bengali, social studies, mathematics, and science. The school day begins at ten in the morning and ends at four in the afternoon. Before school begins, I usually spend an hour studying my lessons. I must also look after my sisters before I go off to class. When I come home from school in the afternoon, I have a late lunch. Then I can spend the rest of the afternoon playing with my friends. Later I help my mother with the cooking and other household chores." Prathiva fetches the water for the family, carrying it from the well in a big kettle. The clay pot she uses is called a *kalshi*. Dinner is at ten o'clock.

For all three meals the family diet centers on rice. They do not eat *chapatis*, the typical Punjabi food, similar to a tortilla. Even for breakfast they eat rice. Since they eat no red meat, they might have vegetable curries. When they can afford it, they have a chicken curry, but because of their religious beliefs, they eat no mutton or beef. Some Hindus do eat mutton, but among the *sanatans*, the sect to which Prathiva's family belongs, it is forbidden.

Twice a year, in January and in March, the village of Sonargaon enjoys a festival. In January they celebrate the feast of Brahma Puti and in March, the feast of Loknath. During these festivals, gifts are offered to the gods. The villagers offer *chita* (a kind of husked, fried rice), *muri* (a popped corn), molasses, and sometimes fruits such as mangoes, bananas, and pineapples. Because they are poor, they cannot afford more than these few things. From the Hindu holy book, called the Bhagavad-Gita, the villagers recite various verses, chosen according to the festival being celebrated.

Marriage is a certainty in Prathiva's mind. "In a few years, when I am of age, I will have a Hindu marriage, arranged by my uncle. Music is very important in a Hindu wedding ceremony." Unlike the more quiet Moslem ceremony, the Hindu marriage takes place in an atmosphere of joy. The wedding feast and the music continue through the night and even through a second day. Prathiva's wedding will be financed by some of her relatives, especially her maternal uncle. The choice of her husband rests with her paternal uncle, who acts as caretaker of her family. This aspect of the Hindu marriage exactly parallels that of the Moslems. Prathiva expects to marry at sixteen or seventeen, like her Moslem friends. This is the traditional Bengali way for Hindu and Moslem alike.

"If my future husband comes from Dacca, then I would be happy to live there. But if he comes from the village and wishes to stay here, then I will stay with him in the village. The choice is completely up to him." Prathiva has seen a little of Dacca. One of her relatives, a member of the National Militia band called the Rakhi Bahini, once took her and her grandmother to Dacca for eight days. Prathiva's views of the big city were very restricted, since she stayed with relatives and rarely left their home. Still, she says, "I was fascinated with the city of Dacca and like it very much."

Prathiva's future and that of Bangladesh unite in their uncertainty. When independence became a reality in March 1971, she expected great security and freedom. The news of independence, heard first by word of mouth, then over the radio, brought her great happiness. But since independence, this jubilance has given way to despair. Inflation makes day-to-day living a constant struggle. Much looting occurs, and people are often robbed at gunpoint. Though Prathiva has not experienced this personally, the story is one she has heard frequently in her own village.

As a Hindu, Prathiva's hopes lie in the continuation of friendly and supportive relations between India and Bangladesh—but even if that relationship should deteriorate, Prathiva and her family intend to remain in Bangladesh until the end of their lives.

---

*Muni, a classmate of Prathiva*

92

# 6

## MAQSUOODA BEGUM
### fifteen
### Housemaid

"On the night of the crackdown, March 25, 1971, the city of Dacca was in flames. There was turmoil all around us and we could hear shells exploding and tanks rumbling by, filled with Pakistani soldiers. We were terrified to see the soldiers shooting people, and so my mother and I fled from the city."

Thus Maqsuooda Begum, a fifteen-year-old housemaid, describes how she began her flight from the war-torn city of Dacca to her native village of Nazimpur in the district of Faridpur. Along with thousands of other fleeing people, Maqsuooda headed for the relative safety of the countryside.

"Ordinarily, if we wanted to go to Nazimpur, we would take the steamer to Savar, and from there a ferry to our village. But during the war there was no steamer service, so we had to go on foot all the way, until the very end." Incredibly, Maqsuooda and her mother covered the fifty miles from Dacca to Savar in just two days, by walking nearly all the time. "We were too terrified to rest in one spot for very long. Although we stopped at night, I was afraid to go to sleep because I knew that the soldiers were all around us. I was frightened of them and thought they would try to rape me."

All along the route, the Punjabi soldiers from Pakistan clashed with insurgents of the East Bengal regiment. Skirmishes could occur anywhere, but Maqsuooda managed to avoid these places, tracing a devious route around the trouble spots.

At the end of the journey, Maqsuooda and her mother found a ferry to cross the river, and they finally made their way to the village. Ironically, upon reaching Nazimpur they discovered the villagers gripped by terror and preparing to leave for a safer place.

"The Pakistani soldiers were advancing on the village, coming closer and closer. Everyone was moving around from village to village, trying to stay away from the army. When the soldiers came into our village to carry out their operations, my friends and I and the other people would hide in the jute fields. The jute trees grow to about fifteen feet high and make good hiding places." At the first sign of danger, Maqsuooda would quickly jump into the muddy paddies. As soon as the soldiers were gone and it was safe to come out, she would wash off all the mud from the paddy and wait for the next action. This constant hide-and-go-seek, played for the highest stake, one's life, occurred throughout the war. The district of Faridpur, one of the main targets of the Pakistani Army, was singled out for its symbolic value as the native district of Prime Minister Sheik Mujib. The soldiers constantly conducted search operations in the area, looking for Mukti Bahini.

"Throughout the war of liberation, while I was staying in the village, I lived in constant terror. At night I was always worried about being kidnapped and this often kept me awake. I thought that if the Pakistani soldiers came at night, and I was awake and alert, I could escape and hide."

Maqsuooda's fears were based on what she saw of the soldiers' savagery in her own village. "Several people were shot to death and left on the street. I could see their gun-shot wounds. Several times I saw dead men floating in the river. And I knew that about twenty girls from the village had been taken by the soldiers and raped." Most of these were schoolgirls, about sixteen or seventeen years old. Some were raped in the village, while others were taken away to the army camps. All of them disappeared from the village life, never to be seen again. A few are thought to have survived, but they will never reappear in the village. Their shame would be too great for them to try to resume their accustomed place in society. In some areas of the country, a rehabilitation program was set up to help women such as these. Those who were successfully rehabilitated were re-

turned to their villages. Unfortunately, they are far outnumbered by the women who did not receive this care and attention.

Though too shy to discuss any details of the stories she had heard about these girls, Maqsuooda showed that she was well aware of the implications of the word "rape." Her bitterness over this tragedy is compounded by the knowledge that local villagers collaborated with the soldiers.

"The soldiers were aided in their terrible deeds by some of the men from the village. Our fellow Bengalis worked with the soldiers, pointing out the attractive young girls and showing where they lived. We think that the collaborators even participated in the rape of some of the girls. There was no peace of mind for anyone in our village during the war. Our own neighbors could have been collaborators of the enemy."

Long before the 1971 war of independence, Maqsuooda and her mother had begun to fight their own private war against poverty and deprivation. Until she was nine years old, Maqsuooda had lived happily with her family in Nazimpur. Suddenly some mental illness took hold of her father and he disappeared. To this day he remains a missing person, although Maqsuooda thinks and hopes that he is still alive. The family had no income after he was gone, so Maqsuooda's uncle arranged for her mother to become a housemaid in the home of a government officer in Dacca.

"Before we came to Dacca to work, I had never been out

of our village. When we arrived in the city, I thought I was in a dreamland. I could not believe that men had constructed the big buildings, or that there could be so many cars. Life in our village was simple, but in Dacca the people had so many different attractions available. I was astonished by everything I saw. My mother and I went sightseeing all over the city in the first few days, on foot. I thought that in such a glorious city we would be able to get employment easily and make a lot of money."

This dream of easy employment and good earnings quickly clashed with reality. Although only wealthy people in Bangladesh can afford servants, the wages they pay are miserably low. At the government officer's house, where Maqsuooda's mother began working as a housemaid, she was paid fifteen

*taka* a month (two dollars), plus room and board. Maqsuooda stayed with her mother and worked as a baby-sitter. Although only nine years old herself, Maqsuooda was expected to look after younger children of the household. In Bangladesh it is not unusual for children of six or seven years of age to have some responsibility for their younger brothers and sisters. Though functioning as an unpaid assistant, Maqsuooda was already starting to support herself by working for her room and board. This arrangement continued for three years.

When she was twelve, Maqsuooda got her first independent job as a live-in housemaid, at a salary of five *taka* a month. For the first time, she found herself completely cut off from her family. Unable to adjust to being on her own, she felt terribly lonely and cried nearly all the time. Within a month, the family employing her had had its fill of this miserable, lonely child and sent her back to her mother.

Instead of trying to find other work for her, Maqsuooda's mother decided that she would be better off caring for her young brother and sister, who were living in a house a few miles outside Dacca. For several months, Maqsuooda was a substitute mother to them, cooking, and seeing that they washed properly and went to bed. This arrangement ended when the children were taken home to Nazimpur to stay with other relatives.

By now Maqsuooda was mature enough to work on her own, and she began a new job, in Dacca, as a housemaid in the home of a Bengali engineer. Her salary was seven *taka* a month. Maqsuooda remained in this job for two years, until the outbreak of war in 1971. At that time, she and her mother began their trek back to their village. The engineer for whom she was working also went into hiding.

After independence, Maqsuooda stayed in Nazimpur for a year, again looking after the younger children of the family.

Once back in Dacca, she found employment in the home of a young widow, a woman whose husband was one of the several hundred leading intellectuals murdered in the last days of the war. The building in which she lives is populated entirely by such widows and their children. Not only did these women lose their husbands but the nation lost many of its finest minds.

"I get up very early in the morning. Before breakfast, I sweep, dust the furniture, and clean the bathroom. For breakfast I usually have *chapatis*. After breakfast, I have to wash the clothes for the whole family—six people—and myself. The memsahib [lady of the house] prepares lunch for the family and they eat together. Then I wash the dishes. After that I usually have a shower and then I eat a late lunch. When I am finished, I have an hour to myself. During the afternoon I look after two young children, taking care of them and going outside to play with them. When it is nearly dark, I go back to the house to help prepare dinner. After dinner, I wash the dishes again. The work is really very hard and the hours are so long."

In spite of all the work Maqsuooda does, her employer is

not satisfied. She often scolds and complains about her work, which makes Maqsuooda very unhappy. And she earns only twelve *taka* a month. She hopes to find a better-paying job and improve her working conditions. Because she cannot look for another job—if her employer found out, hostility in the household would be increased—Maqsuooda's mother is trying to find one for her. Until she is able to make a change, she must silently bear her burden. Almost more important than an increase in salary is Maqsuooda's desire to find a more pleasant family to work for.

In hiring a servant, a family considers the character of the potential employee very carefully. Honesty is the quality uppermost in the mind of the employer. Once that is established, a wage is offered, based on the amount of work to be done. This depends on the size of the family, on whether or not the servant is to go marketing, on whether or not she knows how to cook. All these considerations are weighed before an offer is made.

At the age of fifteen, Maqsuooda is attending school for the first time. Inspired by the example of other housemaids, she requested and received permission to attend a free school for one hour a day. Each day she studies her Bengali primer, called *Sabuj Sathi*. She is learning to read and write Bengali and hopes to continue her schooling. But this meager education will not free Maqsuooda from her occupation as a housemaid.

In addition to her small salary, Maqsuooda is given her

room and board and, on special occasions, some clothes. Such an occasion might be Eid, the most important Moslem festival, which follows a full month of fasting. At this time, people visit one another and prepare a special feast. Maqsuooda might be given a sari or some silver ornaments to wear. And occasionally during the year she receives a small bonus of money called baksheesh.

For Maqsuooda, the future holds only one choice: marriage. She must continue to work as a housemaid for a very poor wage and hope to make a good marriage. This will lift her out of the servant class and give her a life of her own, no matter how poor.

The possibility exists that Maqsuooda's marriage might be

a love match, rather than arranged. She has a certain amount of freedom because she spends part of the day outside with the children and has a slight chance of meeting a boy in that way.

More likely, Maqsuooda's mother will present a marriage candidate to her. Since she has an unusually friendly relationship with her mother, however, her own desires will be taken into consideration, more so than in the typical lower-class family. But her mother will have the ultimate say in her marriage.

Once married, Maqsuooda expects her life to be quite different. "I will observe purdah [the traditional sheltered life of women in Bangladesh] according to my future husband's wishes. I will stay in the house most of the time, and when I go out, I will wear the veil [a heavily concealing garment covering the entire body]. And I must become much more serious about religion or my husband will think that I am an infidel, and not a good Moslem. So I will spend time saying my prayers properly and not anger my husband."

So Maqsuooda will end her unhappy time as a housemaid and enter the traditional closed world of marriage. For a practically illiterate, poor, fifteen-year-old girl, marriage is the only choice.

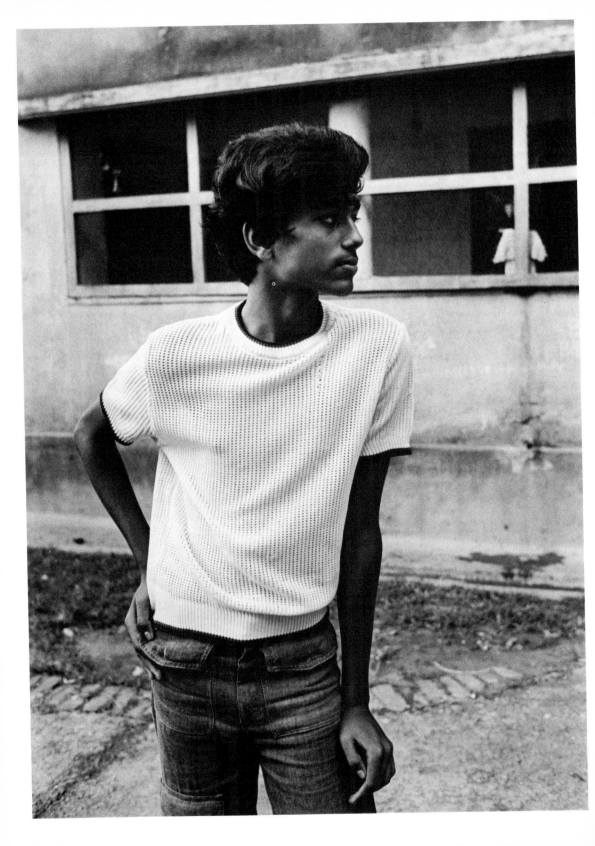

# 7

## MISHUK MUNIER
### thirteen
### Middle-class boy

In the last bitter days of the war, the al-Bahadur, a fanatically religious group of Bengali Moslems, embarked on its senseless massacre, rounding up three hundred intellectuals, torturing and killing most of them. In this one stroke, the new nation was deprived of the best of its educated class.

A leading intellectual who fell prey to this last desperate attack was Munier Chowdhury, father of Mishuk, a thirteen-year-old schoolboy. All the advantages seem to surround Mishuk. In a land where the thread of life is very, very thin, he has no worries about where his next meal will come from. His education is assured, and he has plenty of time to enjoy sports activities. But the cloud that hangs over him is as sad as the poverty that affects his countrymen, for he can never forget how he lost his father.

"I was standing on the balcony of our house when suddenly I saw *razakars* coming to our door. They marched in and took my father away. I remember that some were wearing uniforms and others were in civilian clothes, but they all had guns. There was nothing I could do. My mother was sitting with my little brother on her lap and she was weeping. My poor grandmother cried as she watched her son being hurried away. We were in shock to think of my father gone. And from that day, December 14, 1971, we never saw him again."

Mishuk's father had taken a big gamble by staying in Dacca at this time, because he had suspected for some while that he might be taken prisoner. But he was powerless to leave the city. In the 1950's, his health had been permanently crushed by a term in jail for intellectual "crimes." The inhuman prison conditions left him crippled with arthritis of the spine, which prevented him from making his escape through the arduous "underground" route.

"Back in October, my father considered leaving in spite of his health, but he said, 'Why should I go now? Freedom is almost at hand. We have nothing to fear.' But he was terribly wrong. A few days before he was taken, atrocities were committed at other places in Bangladesh. We had no way of knowing about that and were not warned of the danger in time."

Mishuk's father was one of the best-known literary figures in the country. Before his son was born, he headed the department of English at Dacca University. In 1952 a colleague persuaded him to undertake the teaching of Bengali. Urdu was then the official language of Pakistan and the government severely repressed the use of Bengali. As head of the department of Bengali at the university, Munier Chowdhury represented the strongest opposition to the government's policy and he was imprisoned for his language work. At the time of his capture in 1971, he was a member of the writers' guild and director of the Bangla academy, dedicated to perpetuating the Bengali language and culture.

For Mishuk, his father's intellectual achievements were overshadowed by the warmth and loving care he showed him. "I would say that he was different from other fathers that I have seen. He cared for everyone. He visited my grandmother every day after leaving the university. I came home from school before he did and I would wait for him to take me out. I loved to go in a car, and wherever he went, he would take me. We were so close. I loved him more than anything."

To this day, Mishuk tries not to think that his father is dead. Because the body has not been found, he can cling to this hope. But many of the three hundred intellectuals picked up between December 12 and 16 were found afterward, their hands tied behind them, tortured and mutilated beyond recognition.

"They did this out of hatred, as a last-moment do-or-die move. Perhaps they thought that India would win, and so if we were independent, that would create an intellectual vacuum. We are without the services of the cream of the country. We have lost many of our great men and all this brutality accomplished nothing."

With his father gone, Mishuk's life today centers around his schooling. Potentially he is one of the future intellectuals of the country, and his sight is fixed firmly on completing the first ten school grades and then going on to higher education.

"I begin classes at 8:30 in the morning and continue until 1:40 in the afternoon, with a half-hour break for a bite to eat. We have seven classes a day, each one forty minutes long." By the ninth grade, as in the British educational system, each student has already chosen his future course in either arts or sciences. This early decision contrasts with most educational systems, which give students a broad range of subjects until they complete the first twelve grades. Mishuk's classmates follow separate programs, although they are united for general work.

Mishuk's language courses include both the literary and technical use of language. His English class studies poetry and prose, letter writing, grammar, and so on. It is conducted in English, although the teacher also speaks Bengali for complete comprehension. All other classes are taught in Bengali, which was the language of instruction even before liberation. Mishuk is quite fluent in English and conversed easily with the author. Before liberation, Mishuk was required to study Urdu as well.

In Mishuk's school, girls study in a separate classroom.

Other Bengali schools allow boys and girls to study in the same room, but they are separated in seating, with boys and girls sitting on different, long benches. Mishuk attends classes six days a week, including Saturday. Students in grades one through six go to school five days a week. He enjoys a month-long summer vacation from the middle of May through the middle of June.

Because of his family's impressive achievements in literature, drama, and communications, Mishuk's future course is inevitable. When he has completed his studies, he thinks

he would like to become a journalist. There is a strong journalistic tradition in Bangladesh.

Twice a month Mishuk and several other schoolchildren participate as panelists on a radio program, discussing subjects of interest to their contemporaries. He is paid a small sum for his part in the program. This activity is part of the family tradition, because his mother has been a well-known actress since the 1940's, also appearing on television.

Once he earns his degree at Dacca University, Mishuk wants to broaden his educational horizons. Most likely he will travel to New Delhi in India, where his older brother Bhashon currently studies theater arts and where Mishuk could take a graduate degree.

Mishuk strongly feels the gaps left in the nation's intellectual life. Both personally and as a citizen, he suffers the loss of the massacre of the intellectuals, a loss heightened by the continuing emigration of the educated young, who see no future for themselves in Bangladesh.

Though only thirteen, Mishuk is thoroughly dissatisfied with conditions in the nation. "Everywhere I go, there's something wrong. There's dishonesty everywhere. In the examination halls, so many people cheat." This moral breakdown, however, did not begin with the war. Mishuk is too young to know that these conditions prevailed well before 1971 and that the fighting only aggravated them.

His view is strongly colored by his personal tragedy. "If this had not happened to my family, I could enjoy the freedom of Bangladesh much more. But because of this loss, I feel no share in the new nation. My father meant everything to my life."

When it comes to inflation, Mishuk has a very different view from most Bengalis, who are constantly beset by the high cost of food. His complaint is far more frivolous.

"To buy something today is very costly. Before the war, it would cost nine or ten *taka* to buy a new cricket ball. Today it's fifty *taka,* and the ball is no good. You drop this ball, it doesn't get up. It stays down. The goods we get now are from India. They're inferior to the goods we got when we were part of Pakistan. Some items like cricket bats are just not available. You can't buy a cricket bat in Bangladesh."

Mishuk enjoys playing cricket and football (soccer) with his friends after school. Whenever the weather is good, they play from four until six-thirty in the afternoon.

He spends part of his time helping his mother in the house because they no longer can afford to have a servant to help. Mishuk dusts and sweeps, and cleans up the table after meals. Sometimes he goes shopping for food. He also feeds his little brother Tonmoy, who is six years old.

For breakfast Mishuk has a very different meal than most of his countrymen. He eats toast with butter and marmalade, eggs, and milk with Ovaltine. Ovaltine is a popular drink in Bangladesh for those who can afford it. Lunch and dinner are typically Bengali: usually rice and chicken with *dal,* and fried vegetables. For dinner, they might have rice, or meat with rice and *chapati.* During his school break, Mishuk goes to the school cafeteria to have milk and a snack. He often

has a meat-filled pastry called *samosa,* shaped like a shell.

Mishuk's schooling was completely disrupted by the civil war. At that time the family was living in his grandfather's house in Dhanmondi, a fine residential section of Dacca. Without warning, the Mukti Bahini appeared and began searching the area. Mishuk was terrified. "We didn't know what was going to happen. Suddenly they blew up a car right on the street and left it in a narrow alley next to our house. We had scarcely recovered from this when the West Pakistani police invaded our neighborhood. We were trapped in an armed camp. Though I didn't know it at the time, the army was also blocking the roads.

"Unaware of this, I had gone to my friend's house to borrow some comic books. He warned me about the police blockade. On the way home, I had just slipped inside the gate when I was scared out of my wits. The police stopped me. First they asked what I had inside my bag. It was only the comic books, but they started poking me for no reason at all. Then one of them kicked me and said, 'Get lost.' I was shaking when I got inside my house."

In December, when the war broke out, Mishuk heard the Indian planes attacking. "I was awakened suddenly. I didn't understand exactly what was going on. Everyone in my family came down to the first floor and I found them talking about the Indians coming over. I didn't know what to think of it. During these last two weeks of the war I went out very little. I was not permitted to go anywhere except to a neighbor's house down the road.

"The airport was only four miles away from our house, so the planes would fly exactly overhead. I used to watch them through the leaves of a coconut tree. I saw dogfights between the planes and once someone bailed out. Shortly after, the plane crashed and I could see black smoke coming out. I was constantly afraid that a bomb might fall on the house.

"Although we thought the Indians would win, on the radio the Pakistanis were distorting all the war reports. They would boast that so many Indian planes were shot down and they gave false casualty reports. This was done to mislead us, to persuade us that they were winning, especially at the end. They even bombed hospitals and orphanages and said that the Indians did it. This wasn't just a rumor; some people actually saw it happen."

The many changes in Mishuk's life because of the war and the loss of his father have turned him away from his faith. Although nominally a Moslem, he does not practice his religion any more. Mishuk's religious training began in school and continued through the sixth grade. The history of the beginning of the Moslem religion is a story every schoolchild hears.

There are two main sects in the Moslem faith, the Sunnis and the Shias. Mishuk and his family are Sunnis—that is, they base their religious belief on not only the teachings of the Koran and the recorded thoughts of the Prophet, Mohammed, but oral traditions too. The Shias, who reject the oral

*One of the Mukti Bahini, a freedom fighter*

traditions but follow the teachings in the Koran, venerate as martyrs the two grandsons of the Prophet, Hasan and Husain. Every year, to commemorate the anniversary of the killing of Husain at a place called Karbala, the Shias observe a time of mourning, during the month of Muharram. They chant slogans and beat their chests to recall this evil deed. Most of the people in Bangladesh are Sunnis, while those in Pakistan are Shias. This division reinforces the separateness of the two former parts of Pakistan.

Attendance at public religious observances at the mosque is limited to men. Some beggar women stay outside, just within the grounds, but they are not permitted inside the building.

Eid, the most important religious festival, occurs twice a year. The first celebration, immediately after Ramadan, the month of fasting, is called Eid-ul-azah and is a time for rejoicing and feasting. The second, Eid-ul-zoha, is a more serious observance that involves the ritual sacrifice of animals.

In Mishuk's school, Moslems, Christians, and Hindus mix freely. Religious class is held at the end of the school day so that those who wish to leave may do so. The Moslem religion is emphasized in class; very little is taught about Hinduism.

Mishuk wears either Western or traditional Bengali clothes. Twice a week there is a school assembly when everyone is supposed to wear the school uniform—navy-blue trousers and a light-blue shirt with a white stripe. Each student must supply his own uniform. Before the war, the outfit cost about forty *taka*. Since the price is now one hundred *taka*, school officials have relaxed the regulation and merely encourage students to comply with the regulation as closely as possible. At home, and while sleeping, Mishuk wears the *lungi*, a traditional Bengali garment.

Western influences—clothes, food, language—play a large role in Mishuk's daily life. He is part of the tiny middle class in Bangladesh and, as such, is one of the bright hopes of the country's future. Mishuk feels great frustration living in Bangladesh today. He sees much that is wrong, such as the inflation that makes daily life a constant struggle. If the country goes on this way, he sees no good in staying. Yet he wants to see change. "I think everyone wants to stand on his own. I pray and I hope that they will do it themselves and not need anyone's help. I want to live happily here."

# 8

## SHELLY GOMES
### eleven
### Orphan girl

For an orphan, the chance to be adopted is usually a passport to a happy family life. But for Shelly Gomes, adoption meant the start of a life without love or affection.

When she was two months old, her parents died. She was brought to a convent at Chittagong, where she lived until she was about four. A childless couple adopted her, but their unhappy marriage could not bear the additional burden she placed on it. Because the family lived in a state of extreme poverty, Shelly strained their financial situation to the breaking point. They would often hit her and insult and rebuke her, especially during meals. "There was no peace in the household for me and I ran away. Now I live in a happier, more pleasant home."

Shelly's new home was found for her by a priest when she

was about eight and was again living in the convent. The priest knew of a large family that needed a girl to look after the children. Shelly's second foster parents live with many of their relatives, in an extended-family situation. She is much happier here, though she works very hard.

Shelly's principal responsibilities are to look after the children of one couple. Her foster mother, a schoolteacher, leaves her in charge of the little ones. Though only eleven years old, Shelly acts as their mother, feeding, soothing, and in general taking care of them while their mother is away.

Shelly went to school while she was with her first foster parents, the only benefit she enjoyed with them. Now, when she should be in school, she must work, so her formal education ended at the age of eight.

"Not only do I have to work with the children, I am always on call to almost everyone in this large family. I wash the dishes and do the clothes of the small children. I also work around the house." Shelly often feels unhappy with her tasks. When she is most upset, she likes to be alone, just to be away from all the chores and the people.

"The thing I enjoy most is singing and performing the classical Indian dance I learned in school." In the missionary schools that are typical of the country, lessons in singing and dancing are a common part of the curriculum. With her friends in the village—Mohtbari, a few miles from Dacca —Shelly likes to perform these dances.

Though Shelly has had some schooling, she is not really

literate. Her life is a simple one, as limited as that of most of her countrymen. Only once has she been to a movie, and television is unknown to her. But she is very fortunate because, unlike many young people in Bangladesh, she does not suffer for want of food, clothes, or shelter. Though she works very hard for a young girl, her life is not a constant search for something to eat.

Shelly has few possessions to call her own. She has two simple dresses. When she wants to wear a sari, the traditional dress of the country, she must borrow it from her foster mother. All saris are the same length and can be draped to fit anyone, young or old.

She thinks she was better off before liberation. During the war she was just nine years old. "I would hear people talking about the liberation, but I was too young to understand much. I thought that a bomb might fall on our house and that I might die. When I saw planes coming near, I was terribly afraid."

During the war, Shelly's foster parents helped the Mukti Bahini, giving them rice and money. The area was fairly safe from guerrilla activity, anyway, because the enormous water lilies in the local streams prevented Pakistani soldiers from using their speedboats. Many Bengalis took shelter in this area, where the people were sympathetic to the Mukti Bahini and so enjoyed relative safety.

The story of Cinderella comes to mind when one considers Shelly's life. Here is a pretty girl doing all the household chores while her unattractive foster sisters don't have to work at all. For Shelly, a Prince Charming is the only realistic way out of her present drudgery.

Her future lies in marriage, in an arranged marriage whose rituals are centuries old. Though she denies she is thinking about marriage when she is asked, this too is part of the elaborate ritual. It is not considered feminine or proper for a girl to think or talk about marriage. Actually, there is little else for her to think about. Whether she is rich or poor, marriage is her destiny. She may talk about it with her friends, but not with her parents or guardians. Although Shelly is a Christian, the rituals that govern her marriage arrangements are virtually identical to those of her Moslem contemporaries.

When Shelly is about fourteen years old, her foster parents will begin to think about her marriage. The same is true of a boy, when he is about eighteen. Each set of parents is always aware of the possible candidates for their child.

In educated families it is possible for young people who attend universities to meet and talk with one another, and form attachments that could lead to marriage. But it is considered improper for Shelly to talk to boys she does not know. She is permitted to speak to the boys of the family because she is considered a real family member, even though her adoption was not an official one. In any case, Shelly would have little chance to talk with a boy, except perhaps when she goes to draw water from the well.

Shelly, then, must rely on her foster parents to lead her through the marriage rituals. Although they may have certain candidates in mind, they must wait for the parents of the boys

to come to them with a proposal. After they receive it, they will consider the boy—his personal behavior, his income or potential income. While this is going on, and especially if there is more than one proposal being offered, Shelly will not be made part of the discussions. She is not permitted to ask questions, either. Once a decision is made by her foster parents about a young man, they will discuss it with her. If she is opposed to their selection for some reason, they will try to find out why.

If Shelly became interested in another boy, perhaps through her friends, she would not tell her foster parents about this directly. She might tell another close relative, such as an aunt or sister-in-law, or if she were bold enough, she could tell the boy to ask his father to make a proposal to her foster parents. This would be an honorable way of setting the wheels in motion.

When both fathers have come to a tentative agreement, the boy will be asked to the house so that Shelly can meet him. Her foster parents will tell her that they have collected enough information about the young man to believe that he is a good person, of a respectable family.

Of course, the candidate must be of the same faith as the girl. There is total disapproval of any religious intermarriage, whether the combination be between Hindu and Moslem, Hindu and Christian, or Christian and Moslem. If a girl marries out of her religion, she is completely cut off from her family. In such a case, the couple would live in the boy's

home. The girl would often be excommunicated from her church or religious group.

The girl's family generally pays for the cost of the wedding, unless the boy's family is very well to do. Since Shelly's foster parents have assumed total responsibility for her well-being, they would bear the wedding expenses. The wedding can be simple or quite elaborate, depending on the circumstances of the family. If the girl is not very desirable, a young man might make very extensive demands for material goods. In the city, he would ask to be sent abroad for higher education. It is a popular saying that if a man has an ugly daughter, he had best be rich in order to marry her off!

Shelly knows that her future depends on the attitude of her foster parents. If she behaves properly and does her work well, she will be allowed to stay with her family until she is of marriageable age.

Although no one expects her to marry a rich boy, they hope to be able to find a suitable candidate, a farmer or the son of a farmer. A young man in this position would be able to support his wife and bring her to his father's home to live. Many young people spurn life on a farm as demeaning. They dream of completing their education and going to work in an office in Dacca, where, unfortunately, many of them become part of the faceless crowd of petty office workers. They toil as third- or fourth-grade employees of the government, desperately trying to support themselves. They attempt, on meager incomes, to combat the inflated prices of the city, and end up living in poverty.

A farmer's son, on the contrary, can make a living from his land and be home with his wife. He can afford to have a family. So a farmer is the likely husband for Shelly—and fortunately for Shelly and her foster father, she is a very pretty girl.

When Shelly does marry, her life will not be very different from what it is today. She is really preparing for her future role as wife and mother. She will continue to follow the custom of eating separately from the men, but now that she is nearly of marriageable age, she will join her foster mother at meals.

Shelly is extremely fortunate in having her future assured in this way, for to be an orphan in a country where so much of life depends on family relationships can mean having no future at all.

# 9
## SHAMSUL HUQ
### eleven
### Country-boat boy

When the Awami League, the political party of Sheik Mujib, was looking for a symbol that would immediately identify it as the party of the people, it chose the country boat. This simple boat, propelled by hand, forms a vital part of the transportation system of Bangladesh. The flat, water-laced countryside is customarily traveled by country boat; during the season of the southwest monsoons (the time of heavy rains), in June, July, and August, it becomes virtually the only way to cross the country.

For Shamsul Huq, an eleven-year-old country-boat boy, the boat simply provides a pleasant way to make a living. He knows nothing of the symbolism of his wooden boat. His days, each just like the last, are filled with trips back and forth across the river at Savar.

Shamsul works on the boat with his father, Nalu Bepari. A boatman for forty years, his father owns the boat they use. It represents an investment of 450 *taka* (sixty dollars). Although the boat was a major investment for him, it is not constructed of the best-quality wood. He and Shamsul must bail it out constantly. For a fine-quality boat, one that would last as long as thirty years, they would have had to pay more than they could accumulate. So they settled for this boat, and although it is only two years old, already it is leaking noticeably. When the day comes that the boat leaks too fast to bail it out, they will chop it up for firewood and cook their meals over the fire! Then Shamsul's father will buy a new boat. This happens about every five years.

The Huqs live in the village of Ahuyla in a pukka house with brick walls and a tin roof. Of the six brothers and two sisters in the family, only one brother and one married sister live at home. The small house has three rooms including the kitchen, with the toilet located about a hundred yards away. For drinking water they walk about half a mile from the house to a well. For washing their clothes and taking baths, they use a pond close to the house.

Shamsul's day begins at seven o'clock, when he gets up and has his breakfast. He might have any one of a number of different things for breakfast: *muri* (popped corn), *chita* (fried husked rice), or *chapati* with molasses. "Although my main job is as a boat boy, I am also partly responsible for the cows. I spend an hour or so a day looking after them. At about ten o'clock, my father and I walk together to the ferry ghat and begin our boat service."

For the most part the Huqs' boat serves as ferry, taking passengers back and forth across the river. For this trip they charge four *annas* (the equivalent of one fourth of a *taka*, about five cents). Each day they earn about twenty-five *taka*, working until late at night. On Sundays they can earn as much as forty *taka*.

"Occasionally my father and I take passengers all the way to Dacca. This is a very big trip for us. It takes us a whole day to travel from Savar to Dacca." For the trip they charge fifty *taka* for the whole boat. They can take as many as thirteen people on the tiny boat, but if there are any goods to be carried, then they have to take fewer passengers. If they start out at seven in the morning, they reach Dacca by evening. The boat is propelled with long poles that are thrust into the river bottom. Then the boatman pushes on the pole, at the same time lifting it off the bottom. (The author tried to imitate this movement and nearly went into the water with the pole! It is deceptively simple-looking, but quite difficult to do.)

"Once we arrive in Dacca, we must wait until morning to return, so we spend the night on the boat. We rarely find any passengers who want to return to Savar from Dacca, although sometimes we have a boatload of goods to carry."

The full-day trip to Dacca is about fifteen miles. If the Huqs perform ferry service only, they cover about the same

fifteen miles' distance during the course of the day. On the return trip from Dacca, they can put up a sail and take advantage of the favorable wind. This speeds up the trip home and also makes it a little easier for them.

Going to Dacca, though, is very much out of the ordinary routine, being a trip that they might not make for months. And for this trip, Shamsul could not work alone. It is beyond his capacity to control the boat, since they must cross a major river during the journey.

"For the usual trips across the small river, I can work the boat alone. If people want to go to their villages and to the markets, I can pole the boat with some passengers for three or four miles, if the current is not too strong. When there is a strong current, though, I cannot go even half a mile alone. Then I must have my father's help."

During a regular day, Shamsul works until one or two o'clock in the afternoon and then stops for lunch. He returns to his house for a meal of rice and fish curry with *dal*. Along with this he may have *bharta*, a dish made of boiled potato, mashed with chili, onion, oil, and salt. This is mixed together and then eaten with the rice. After this meal, Shamsul returns to the boat, working as late as nine o'clock or sometimes even until ten or eleven. After this very long workday, he returns home for dinner, generally rice and a curry with *dal*.

For three years Shamsul has been following his trade as a boatman. He has never been to school, although most of his friends go. Shamsul has never been exposed to any schooling in his own family, all of whom are illiterate. But he has no

141

desire to be in school. He is a sort of Huckleberry Finn who enjoys his freedom of movement on the boat, his life as a free spirit.

"It is my great ambition to own a boat like my father and maybe someday to have my own little fleet of such boats. I think that when I am twenty-five years old, I will have much greater strength. And then I hope I will have the courage to face the ordeal of the river, to be able to ply a boat in a stormy night. This strength and confidence, I think, will come by the time I am twenty-five."

At present Shamsul does not receive a salary or allowance from his father for his work on the boat. Until he is ready to buy his own boat, he expects to continue his present arrangement. But when the time does come to buy a boat, he is confident that his father will have the money to lend him for the purchase. After he buys his first boat, he intends to work and save until he can buy a second. Then he would hire someone to work that boat and eventually buy another, and so on. This is his master plan. Although Shamsul has had a taste of Dacca, he does not enjoy city life. "When Father and I stay in Dacca overnight, I think all the time only of coming back to the village, to be with my friends and to be working on the boat." Shamsul is a true village boy who enjoys being on his home ground.

For the three months of the southwest monsoon season, Shamsul and his father work their hardest. Once the rains pass, though, the rivers begin to recede and sometimes they

142

cannot pole the boat in the shallow water. In those quieter months, Shamsul spends more time looking after the cows and tilling the land, doing odd jobs around the house.

During the month of December, they sow their three bighas of land with *irri* rice. At other times of the year they grow vegetables and mustard seeds for oil. Although Shamsul helps out in the fields, they are mainly worked by his fifteen-year-old brother, the farmer of the family. The division of labor was arranged by their father and it pleases Shamsul, because he much prefers to work on the boat.

Shamsul's brother also looks after their three cows. The milk from the cows is sold in the market, bringing in about

four to five *taka* each day. So the family has earnings from both the water and the land. They grow some of their food and supply their own milk, making them an unusually self-sufficient family.

Though Shamsul expects to have his own boat when he is twenty-five, he plans to marry somewhat earlier, at about twenty-two or twenty-three. He has no worries about supporting his future wife, whom he expects to bring to his parents' home, to form a joint family. Shamsul does not consider establishing a household of his own. "I will marry a girl chosen for me by my parents. I am sure I would be very happy with the girl whom my parents select for me." Shamsul says he expects his wife to observe purdah. She will stay indoors and wear the veil. And he expects her to be an obedient wife. What Shamsul says about marriage and how his wife would behave may change radically when he grows older. His view now is that of an eleven-year-old country boy.

During the war of liberation, Shamsul's village was in a very strategic location. The river, one of the main arteries of the country, and its surrounding area were under heavy attack by the Pakistani Army. During the war Shamsul saw many atrocities committed in his own village. Houses were burned and people were killed. Although no one in his own family was affected, they were forced to flee their village and move from place to place, trying to avoid confrontation with the Pakistani Army. During the final two weeks, when India joined the battle, a few bombs were dropped near his village,

by the Indian Army, which was trying to uproot the Pakistani concentration in certain pockets of the area. The ferry ghat where the Huqs kept their boat was under Pakistani control during the war.

During this time, Shamsul recalls, "I would pray for the salvation of the Bengali nation. I would pray for the freedom of Bangladesh. I was so happy when the new flag of Bangladesh was hoisted in my village, on December 16, 1971."

Shamsul expected a better life for himself and his family under this new regime, in the new nation of Bangladesh, but his expectations have not materialized. "All I see instead are rising prices of all the essential goods—food, clothing, and everything necessary to life. And I am afraid of the very frequent robberies that we hear about in the village." Crime has increased greatly in the country as a whole and Shamsul is afraid of attack or that his house might be robbed.

Yet his possessions are few. Since he doesn't read, he has no need for books. All he owns are two *lungis*, one pair of trousers, two shirts, and one sweater for playing *hadodo*, a local village game. It is a body-contact sport, played in an area like a tennis court, in which two teams of six players each attempt to cross over a central point on the court. It is the game played where the children have no football, no cricket, no badminton, no hockey. It is a game for which one needs no resources other than one's own body. When Shamsul is free of his farm and boat-boy duties, this is the game he likes to play with his friends.

146

So Shamsul sees his daily life stretching out into the years ahead. He sees his marriage planned and arranged by his parents, and his fleet of boats growing steadily in the future.

Only one element has not been foreseen. Shamsul's father is now sixty years old. By the time Shamsul is ready for marriage and boat ownership, according to his own schedule, his father will be in his seventies. The life expectancy in Bangladesh is so low that such planning is scarcely realistic. But for the moment, Shamsul is an eleven-year-old Huck Finn, plying his boat on the river, living from day to day.

# Afterword

On February 22, 1974, a little more than two years after the fall of Dacca and the surrender of the Pakistanis, the nation of Bangladesh was recognized by Pakistan. Bangladesh immediately followed suit, recognizing its former enemy. With these political maneuvers, the nations of the subcontinent took the first steps toward resumption of important travel, communications, and diplomatic links.

The task of reconstruction, begun after independence, moves forward slowly. During the war the nation lost much of the little it had. For the immediate future, Bangladesh faces continuing inflation, food shortages, and rampant corruption.

With a literacy rate of less than 20 percent and nearly the lowest per capita income in the world, the nation has few weapons to carry on its fight against hunger and poverty.

However, the first five-year plan realistically accepted these problems and charted a reconstruction program with modest goals. The country's major export, jute, has risen in value because of shortages of synthetic fibers. If Bangladesh can achieve prewar levels of jute production, she will regain an important source of revenue.

The nearly ten million refugees who flooded into India during the war have all returned to their homeland, while 90,000 Pakistani prisoners of war have been released from Indian camps and returned to Pakistan. Arrangements are being made for an undetermined number of Biharis to be settled in Pakistan.

Education is the key to the future of the children. When the government's plan to provide free schooling through the tenth grade takes effect, more children will achieve literacy and reach higher levels of learning than did their parents. They have hope and they have dreams.

Momin Ullah dreams of his own fleet of rickshaws, while Shamsul Huq envisions himself the owner of several boats. Shahida Begum's hopes are pinned to the success of her brother's career as a mechanic. In April 1974 Pakistan agreed to accept those Biharis who have family links in West Pakistan, so Sarwar Ali, who has an uncle in West Pakistan, may well realize his dream of emigrating there with all his family.

These children are the first generation in Bangladesh—the promise of the nation and its brightest hope.

# Glossary

ANNA  one-sixteenth of a *taka*

ATTA  wheat (either flour or meal)

AWAMI LEAGUE  political party of Sheik Mujib

BANDHU  friend

BANGABANDHU  friend of Bangladesh, specifically Mujib

BIDI  a cheap cigarette of coarse tobacco

BIGHA  a measure of land

BIHARIS  natives of Bihar (a northeastern state of India),
some of whom now live in Bangladesh

BIRANGINAS  the "heroines," specifically, the raped women

CHADDAR  a length of fabric used as a shawl

CHAPATI  flat, unleavened bread made of wheat flour, cooked
on a griddle; similar to a tortilla

CHITTAGONG  second-largest city, largest port, located on
Bay of Bengal

DACCA  capital and largest city

DAL  sauce made from a vegetable like lentils

EID  major religious celebration of Muslims

GHAT  ferry landing, dock

KUTCHA  second-class, inferior, unfinished (structure or object)

LUNGI  a length of cloth wrapped to form a loose garment, worn by boys and men

MEMSAHIB  lady of the house; in direct address: "ma'am"

MONSOON  rainy season marked by torrential rains; occurs for about three months

MUKTI BAHINI  freedom fighters, liberation army

PAISA  currency; about five *paisa* equal one cent

PUKKA  first-class, sturdy (object)

PUNJABI  native of state of Punjab, located partly in West Pakistan, partly in India; name used by Bengalis to refer to all West Pakistani soldiers

PURDAH  traditional secluded life of women; also, the veil (garment covering entire body) or curtains used to screen women from sight

RAZAKARS  collaborators who worked with Pakistanis

SAHIB  gentleman; in direct address, "sir"

SARI  length of cloth wrapped into graceful, long dress

TAKA  unit of money; about 7½ *takas* equal $1

URDU  language of West Pakistanis

WALLAH  person who performs a service